D1572135

"Using the lens of 'adventure,' Daniel Keating presents a wonderfully fresh vision of Christian discipleship. He is equally at home drawing from Scripture, J. R. R. Tolkien, C. S. Lewis, and contemporary adventure tales like *Lost* and *Batman Begins*—appealing especially to young adults who are seeking more in their spiritual life. *The Adventure of Discipleship* is the sort of book that engages, invites, and challenges. You may want to buy several and give them away to your young adult friends."

— MARY HEALY —
Professor of Sacred Scripture, Sacred Heart
Seminary, Detroit, MI

"This book is about true friendship, how to endure suffering, and how to offer our lives to God along the path of real peace. At the same time, drawing upon *The Lord of the Rings*, superhero movies, and other rich storytelling, Keating shows that most of us don't actually want peace—we want our lives to be a meaningful and glorious adventure. The inspiring achievement of this book, then, is to demonstrate that life in Christ provides the peace that is also the greatest possible adventure."

— MATTHEW LEVERING —
James N. and Mary D. Perry, Jr. Chair of Theology,
Mundelein Seminary, Mundelein, IL

"Daniel Keating is an excellent scholar with a keen pastoral sense. His book, *The Adventure of Discipleship*, exemplifies both of these virtues. Keating carefully articulates the story—the adventure—of what it means, in all its various facets, to be a faithful disciple of Jesus Christ and he does so as a man who has lived this journey himself and has pastorally shepherded others to live this venture as well. As all adventures are exciting, so the reading of this book is itself invigorating. One cannot help but be caught up into the adventure of following Christ, no matter what the cost, for one perceives that it is a journey of faith, hope, and love together with Jesus himself. This is an admirable book for those Christians who wish to be more fully Jesus's disciples and an effective book to place in the hands of those who are being evangelized. Both will set out on the grand adventure that is Christianity."

— THOMAS G. WEINANDY, O.F.M., CAP. —
Scholar in Residence at Capuchin College,
Washington, DC, and Former Member of the
Faculty of Theology at Oxford University and of the
Vatican's International Theological Commission

"The sense of adventure has been drowned out in modernity, but an ember remains, ready to burn brightly and engulf us. *The Adventure of Discipleship* reminds us that our lives are a drama so significant that Jesus Christ came into the world to take us on adventure with him. The only adequate response is a no-holds-barred life of discipleship, on mission to bring others into the embrace of Our Lord—and Keating's book helps us begin this adventure!"

— CURTIS MARTIN —
Founder and President, Fellowship of Catholic
University Students (FOCUS)

·❖·

LIVING FAITH

Series Editor: Fr. David Vincent Meconi, S.J.

Fr. David Vincent Meconi, S.J., is a Jesuit priest and professor of theology at Saint Louis University where he also serves as the Director of the Catholic Studies Centre. He is the editor of *Homiletic and Pastoral Review* and has published widely in the areas of Church history and Catholic culture. He holds the pontifical license in Patristics from the University of Innsbruck in Austria, and the D.Phil. in Ecclesiastical History from the University of Oxford.

About the Series

The great Christian Tradition has always affirmed that the world in which we live is a reflection of its divine source, a place perhaps torn apart by sin but still charged with busy and bustling creatures disclosing the beautiful presence of God. The *Living Faith* series consists of eminent Catholic authors who seek to help Christians navigate their way in this world. How do we understand objective truth in a culture insistent on relativism? How does one evangelize in a world offended when invited to something higher? How do we understand sin and salvation when so many have no real interest in becoming saints? The *Living Faith* series will answer these and numerous other questions Christians have today as they set out not only to live holy lives themselves, but to bring others to the fullness of life in Christ Jesus.

Published or Forthcoming

Catholicism and Intelligence
Fr. James V. Schall, S.J.

The Family of God and How Christ Lives in His Church Today
Carl E. Olson

Jesus Christ in Islam and Christianity
Fr. Mitch Pacwa, S.J.

Apologetics and the Christian Imagination
Holly Ordway

Holiness and Living the Sacramental Life
Fr. Philip-Michael Tangorra

The Joyful Mystery: Field Notes Toward a Green Thomism
Christopher J. Thompson

Spirituality of the Business World
Michael Naughton

Sanctity and Scripture
Scott Hahn

Catholic and at College
Anne Carson Daly

*Living Grace & Deadly Sin: A Guide to
Getting Our Souls Straight*
Fr. David Vincent Meconi, S.J.

THE
ADVENTURE
OF
DISCIPLESHIP

THE
ADVENTURE
OF
DISCIPLESHIP

DANIEL A. KEATING

EMMAUS
ROAD
PUBLISHING

Steubenville, Ohio
www.emmausroad.org

Emmaus Road Publishing
1468 Parkview Circle
Steubenville, Ohio 43952

Library of Congress Cataloging-in-Publication Data
Names: Keating, Daniel A., author.
Title: The adventure of discipleship / Daniel A. Keating.
Description: Steubenville : Emmaus Road, 2018. | Series: Living faith |
Includes bibliographical references and index.
Identifiers: LCCN 2018032080 (print) | LCCN 2018033172 (ebook) | ISBN
9781949013252 (e-book) | ISBN 9781949013238 (hard cover) | ISBN
9781949013245 (pbk.)
Subjects: LCSH: Christian life--Catholic authors.
Classification: LCC BX2350.3 (ebook) | LCC BX2350.3 .K43 2018 (print) | DDC
248.4/82--dc23
LC record available at https://lccn.loc.gov/2018032080

Cover image: *The Storm on the Sea of Galilee* (1633) by Rembrandt van Rijn

Cover design and layout by Margaret Ryland

To C. S. Lewis and J. R. R. Tolkien

·❈·

TABLE OF CONTENTS

Acknowledgments   xiii

Introduction: The Gospel as the Costly
                Adventure of Discipleship   1

Chapter 1:   The Anatomy of Adventure   7

Chapter 2:   A Venturesome Faith   29

Chapter 3:   A Costly Discipleship   49

Chapter 4:   RoboCop, Superheroes,
              and the Incarnation   69

Chapter 5:   Providence, Hope,
              and the Gift of the Spirit   87

Chapter 6:   Trials and Suffering in the
              Costly Adventure of Discipleship   113

Chapter 7:   True Friendship in the Adventure
              of Discipleship   135

Chapter 8:   Friendship and
              Communion with God   165

Living the Adventure   189

Bibliography   195

Index of Biblical References   201

Index of Subjects   205

ACKNOWLEDGMENTS

I owe a debt of gratitude to many people who have helped this book reach its final form. Fr. David Meconi approached me and asked if I would consider writing a book for this series. He was, to my surprise, entirely supportive of my proposal to write on the topic of adventurous discipleship in Christ. James Munk sat down with me and helped to craft a topic that would express the heart of what I wanted to say. My brother, Fr. Michael Keating, read through my first draft and offered many helpful suggestions for clarifying and expanding the content of the book. Finally, Chris Erickson, Kate Porter, and Melissa Girard from Emmaus Road Publishing walked me through the editing process and skillfully accompanied the book to publication.

·✦·

The Gospel as the Costly Adventure of Discipleship

If anyone would come after me, let him deny himself
and take up his cross and follow me. For whoever
would save his life will lose it, but whoever loses his
life for my sake and the gospel's will save it.

—Mark 8:34–35, ESV

To hear and believe the good news of Jesus Christ (the
Gospel) is to set out on the costly adventure of discipleship. "Being a Christian" or "becoming a Christian"
involves much more than staking a claim to a religious
identity. It means more than taking on a set of practices
or attending services—though practices and services are
essential. When Jesus says, "Come, follow me," he is inviting us to become his disciples. When we respond to
this call, we leave behind our own plans and enter into
an adventure not of our own making. This adventure of
discipleship is *costly*—it requires the cost of our lives.

Think of Peter and Andrew busily casting their fishing

1

nets into the sea—or James and John mending their nets by the seaside. Jesus walks past and calls them to follow and their lives are never the same (Matt 4:18–22). Or consider Matthew sitting at his tax booth, minding his business. Jesus approaches and says, "Follow me," and Matthew's life is turned upside down (Matt 9:9). Or recall Saul of Tarsus, chasing Christians all the way to Damascus. Jesus reveals himself in blinding light and piercing words, and the arch-persecutor becomes the great Apostle (Acts 9:1–9).

These, of course, are the dramatic stories of the first followers of Jesus. All too easily we bracket them off as exceptional and unique encounters with Jesus, fit only for the first generation. We do the same bracketing of the saints through the ages: these are the especially holy men and women who experienced a dramatic, life-changing encounter with Jesus. Yes, there *is* something exceptional about the first disciples and the saints throughout history. But if we have eyes to see and ears to hear, we recognize that the *kind* of experience they had is a model for us as well. You and I are also given a personal invitation to follow Jesus the Lord on a path of costly, adventurous discipleship.

Why this book? Because in my experience many people, especially young Christians today, lack an imaginative vision of the Christian life. They *reduce* their faith to one of its parts: to a set of beliefs, or to a moral code, or to attending religious services, and so on. These are all essential but they often lack the element of personal discipleship that the Gospels so clearly display. Crucially, we often think about being a Christian primarily as something *we* do, something *we* choose, something that *we* arrange and put in order. We place ourselves in the driver's seat and we construct our life—and our understanding of God—according to our own ideas and preferences. We forge our own religious identity in the same way that we select ingredients from a salad bar.

But this is entirely the wrong way round. The life of a disciple begins when *Jesus* breaks in and calls. We become apprenticed to him and learn from him (and from our fellow disciples) what is true and good and right. He takes us on a path we did not expect to traverse. For sure, our choice is an essential part of this, but it is the choice of whether or not to follow Jesus on his terms. Will we follow as Peter and Matthew did, or will we turn and walk away in sadness like the rich young man?

The thesis of this book is that the adventure of discipleship to Jesus Christ is the true and real story of the world. All other adventures that we create, read, and retell are reflections and refractions of this one great adventure. To become a follower of Jesus Christ is not the private expression of the religious or spiritual side of my personality that I express whenever it suits me. No, becoming a disciple means that we are taken up—swallowed up, really—into Jesus's own life. And it means embarking on a path not of our own making. We are not in charge of the itinerary.

C. S. Lewis, a Christian writer of the twentieth century, recounts a crucial episode in his conversion from atheism to Christianity: it suddenly dawned on him that the story of the Gospel is the true story of the world. Lewis had rejected the Christianity of his youth, but he loved the ancient myths and lived imaginatively inside of them. Through the help of his friends at Oxford (one of whom was J. R. R. Tolkien), Lewis came to recognize that the Gospel of Jesus Christ is actually the "true myth," the real story that all other myths merely reflect. Once Lewis recognized this, many of the obstacles to faith fell away and he was enabled by grace to open himself to the approach of the God he had long been denying.[1]

This book is a product of my own love for adventure. I owe a great debt to C. S. Lewis, J. R. R. Tolkien, and many others who have fed my imagination from early boyhood to the present time. My hope is that by presenting the Christian life in terms of the costly adventure of discipleship, others will be able to see and embrace this adventure for themselves and may be inspired to offer themselves freely and fully to the Lord who is worthy of their whole lives.

I should say at the start that this book is not intended as a primer on every aspect of the Christian faith or a substitute for the Catechism—though the Scriptures, the Creed, and the Catechism are the foundation for everything I will say. Rather, my hope is to describe what it means to be caught up in the costly adventure of following Jesus on the path of discipleship. Along the way I will call upon some of the adventures told (and retold) in our culture today, to show how they help us grasp what it means to be caught up in that great and true adventure of following after Christ. But the most profound examples for us are the holy men and women of the Scriptures and throughout the ages: *the saints*. They exemplify in the most perfect way what it means to follow the path of

---

[1] For Lewis's account of his conversion, see C. S. Lewis, *Surprised by Joy* (New York: HarperCollins, 1955).

costly discipleship. Each chapter, therefore, will conclude with a brief portrait drawn from these saints to serve as a lamppost for us along the path.

The chapters in the book are ordered to give a coherent and connected picture of what it means to follow Christ as his disciples, but each chapter also stands on its own and carries its own message. Readers will profit most by reading the chapters in their given order, but they can also skip over chapters that they find less interesting and still find benefit.

This book is addressed primarily to Catholic readers, and a Catholic understanding of the faith will be assumed throughout. But I have learned much from Orthodox, Anglican, and Evangelical fellow-travelers—I am greatly indebted to them. I hope that what I write will be insightful and inspiring for all Christians—and for anyone who loves adventure.

·✦·

CHAPTER ONE

The Anatomy of Adventure

A man cannot deserve adventures; he cannot earn dragons and hippogriffs.

—G. K. Chesterton[1]

I loved to choose and see my path; but now Lead Thou me on!

—John Henry Newman[2]

THE LOVE OF ADVENTURE

LOVE of adventure comes naturally to us. Children create their own adventures in play all day long—if we let them. Without anyone giving them the script, kids just seem to produce their own stories, characters, plots, and dramatic endings. Good storytellers captivate the attention of

---

[1] G. K. Chesterton, *Heretics* (New York: John Lane, 1909), 70.
[2] John Henry Newman, "Lead Kindly Light," 1834, https://newmanu. edu/about-newman/history-of-newman/lead-kindly-light.

children like nothing else—and the children want to hear the same story again and again.

As a boy, I had two sets of adventure-loving friends. In the first group, we staged intricate "cops and robbers" dramas, running in and out of three neighbors' yards, leaping fences, and hiding in dense shrubbery. In the second group, cowboys and soldiers dominated our imaginary games. With a log cabin, a massive two-story garage, and a labyrinthine basement at our disposal, there was no end to the adventures we could devise. Only the lunch or dinner bell had the power to call us back to the real world.

This form of adventure-making quickly passed away as we grew, but the love of adventure did not die in me. The weekly trip to the local public library brought home a pile of books, and with four older siblings I had a wealth of hand-me-down books on the shelves available to me. The first books that captivated my attention were the Hardy Boys mysteries, but what really fired my imagination were the wilderness adventures of Henry Ware and Paul Cotter, two strapping boys who roamed the Kentucky forests, doing feats of daring and saving their people time and again.[3] I also experienced the delight of hearing my father read aloud *Treasure Island* from cover to cover, and somewhere along the way *Robinson Crusoe* entered my imaginative world.

My tastes were by no means all bookish. Over several years I built up a respectable collection of comic books by

[3] For the wilderness tales of Henry Ware and Paul Cotter, see the eight books of the Young Trailers Series by Joseph Altsheler (written between 1907 and 1917).

making a weekly trip to the local supermarket to see what new editions had appeared. Whether I came across Superman, Batman, Green Lantern, Spiderman, the Fantastic Four, the X-Men, or others, I possessed an endless appetite for the latest superhero who was saving the world. But by the time I reached adolescence, the two great adventures that captured my imagination most of all were the Chronicles of Narnia by C. S. Lewis, and *The Hobbit* and *The Lord of the Rings* by J. R. R. Tolkien. More than any other books, these ignited within me a longing for adventure and a desire for the heroic life.

ESCAPISM OR A LIFELONG DESIRE?

We might think that my experiences as a boy belong to a bygone era that has passed away. To our detriment we have probably lost—to some extent—both the adventure-making games of children and the habit of reading adventure books. But the global phenomenon of Harry Potter shows that the love of adventure is still alive in the millennial generation: young people will still buy and read (lengthy) books that genuinely capture their imagination.

Is this appetite for adventure just a passing phase of youth and adolescence that (rightly) gives way to the realism and responsibility of adulthood? Certainly, the kinds of adventures that animate and enchant us change as we grow. But I contend that the longing for adventure remains alive in adults unless it is thoroughly trampled underfoot. The enormous success of superhero movies attests to this longing for adventure, not just among kids but also in adults. Whether it comes in the form of murder mysteries, science fiction dystopias, or superheroes, we seem to want (and need) a regular supply of adventure to make life worth living. The movie *City Slickers* (1991) nicely captures the drama of an older adult man, shriveling up in his dreary routines, who finds a new motive for living by recapturing an adventurous, risky side of life.[4]

Still, perhaps this thirst for adventure, especially among adults, is just pure escapism. We might say that all this is nothing more than a form of intoxication or medication, to ease the pain and dreariness of normal (real) life. Perhaps Thomas Hobbes was right: human life is "nasty, brutish, and short," and distracting adventure is just one way that we manage our way through. The epic movie *The Matrix* presents one possible way to evaluate our love for adventure: in seeking adventures are we just like the man who chose to be re-plugged into the matrix, artificially escaping from real life by choosing to live in a make-believe world that eases the pain?

In one sense, the stories we listen to and the adventures we create provide an "escape" from our day-to-day lives. For some people this may simply be a way to medicate their pain and withdraw from the demands of life. But this is not necessarily so. The adventures that we love also help us to focus on what is truly real and important. They enable us to see what is good and true and beautiful in new ways. If the stories are full of upright and noble characters, they also encourage the growth of virtue in

---

[4] The thirst for adventure in our culture, especially for men and boys, is demonstrated by the huge success of books such as *The Dangerous Book for Boys* by Conn and Hal Iggulden (2012) and *Wild at Heart* by John Eldredge (2001). Despite whatever shortcomings may be found in these works, they demonstrate a hunger for the adventurous life.

us: they are formative of superior character and habits of mind. Yes, we need catechetical instruction in the Ten Commandments and the cardinal and theological virtues. But we also need to see these commandments and virtues (and the corresponding vices) exemplified in real characters and stories so that we can be inspired to pursue what is good and avoid what is evil.[5] The stories we love help us to see our own lives in a new perspective. They cast a light upon our time on earth that perhaps no other medium can achieve.

More than this, however, I believe that our natural love of adventure—as it develops and matures through life—reveals something important about us. *We were made for an adventurous life.* To say this differently, our lives are best understood as enclosed within a great tale. The adventures that we love are not false to reality but provide so many sketches of the real world in which we live—if we have eyes to see. This brings us to Jesus in the Gospels as the center and climax of the real adventure of our world. But before we pursue this, more needs to be said about the qualities of a real adventure.

ADVENTURE: REAL OR CONTRIVED?

We love adventure but—let's be honest—we like to be in charge of our adventures and arrange them step by step. There is a vast difference between an arranged or contrived adventure, on the one hand, and one that is real

---

[5] In the fourth century, St. Basil the Great, *Address to Young Men on the Right Use of Greek Literature*, offered counsel for how the stories and myths of his era could be profitably used in the formation of young Christians. See https://www.elpenor.org/basil/ancient-literature.asp.

and genuine, on the other. A few examples will display this difference. Some years back I set out on a trip from the United States to London, England. The plans I made constituted my "arranged" adventure and I was very much looking forward to fresh experiences. But when, out over the north Atlantic, one of our two engines failed and the pilot notified us that if he could not restart that engine, we would need to take a left turn and head for Iceland, the real adventure began. Suddenly our lives were in danger, all plans and schedules were off, and we found ourselves in uncharted waters. A loud cheer of relief erupted when we touched down in Reykjavik, and I spent a day touring the city and making new friends that I would not otherwise have met.

On a rainy day in the country, four children—Peter, Susan, Edmund, and Lucy—arranged a game for their entertainment, playing hide and seek in their uncle's old house. The real adventure began when Lucy hid in the wardrobe and found herself in the snowy land of Narnia, right at the center of a titanic battle between the White Witch and Aslan the Lion. The arranged adventure suddenly became a real adventure with life and death on the line. In the movie *City Slickers*, the contrived adventure was going out West to drive a herd of cattle across the country; the real adventure began when the foreman died, the herd stampeded, the hired hands got drunk, and the city slickers had to bring in the herd all by themselves.

Human life is filled with arranged and contrived adventures—and these are by no means bad things. We concoct adventures because our lives have little meaning; we want a measure of excitement and novelty. Usually we arrange these "adventures" so that they are relatively safe and predictable—or at least we keep the "unpredictable" within reasonable bounds. At the end of the day we want to be able to turn off the television, or click on a new link, or close the book and put it on the shelf and be back in our safe, predictable world. This is just how Bilbo the hobbit saw things. When Gandalf appeared at his door and invited him "to share in an adventure" that Gandalf was "arranging," Bilbo promptly declined the offer. "We are plain quiet folk and have no use for adventures. Nasty disturbing uncomfortable things! Make you late for dinner! I can't think what anybody sees in them."[6] Tolkien's readers are immensely grateful that Bilbo did not get his way; despite his efforts to avoid it, he became caught up in a great adventure that changed his life—and the fate of his world—forever.

THE ANATOMY OF A REAL ADVENTURE

Arranged adventures rarely bring us true depth; they are not the stuff of which life is made and characters forged. They are certainly not the kind of adventures we want to read about—and this is telling. The sort of adventures that we all want to read and watch are precisely the *real* ones in which the characters get thrown in over their heads. It is probably impossible to describe with precision the qualities that mark these true and real adventures, the kind that we want to read about, the kind that we dream about being in. But it seems to me that there are some

---

[6] J. R. R. Tolkien, *The Hobbit*, rev. ed. (New York: Ballantine Books, 1966), 4.

common features of great adventures that we can single out. Here I would like to identify three qualities of a true and real adventure.

The first mark of a true and real adventure is that you "land" in it—you don't arrange it or "select" it. A real adventure happens to you; it sweeps you away. In the words of G. K. Chesterton, "an adventure is, by its nature, a thing that comes to us. It is a thing that chooses us, not a thing that we choose."[7] Let us revisit Bilbo Baggins in *The Hobbit*: there he is, sitting quietly in his cozy home, sipping tea and enjoying his peace and quiet. Suddenly there is a knock on the door; in come hordes of dwarves and a wizard, and with no time to prepare or plan, Bilbo is off, running down the road without even handkerchiefs in his pocket. Or consider young Jim Hawkins in *Treasure Island*, minding his mother's inn and living an uneventful life. One day an evil-looking old seaman, Billy Bones, strides in and takes up residence, and everything changes. Before Jim knows it, he is in possession of a treasure map and finds himself on the high seas caught up in a whirlwind of intrigue and murder. He will need all his wits and plenty of luck to survive and come out on top. Or how about young Luke Skywalker, living with his aunt and uncle on an insignificant planet, occupied with dreary and mundane tasks. A "droid" appears with a secret message, the agents of the evil empire follow right behind, and suddenly Luke finds himself at the center of the great battle of his time, slowly learning who he really is, what his powers are, and what he must do to save the universe.

---

[7] Chesterton, *Heretics*, 190.

In *The Two Towers*, J. R. R. Tolkien presents this "unplanned" quality of real adventures through a dialogue between Frodo and Sam as they prepare to enter Mordor in the final stage of the quest. Sam is speaking, musing on their predicament and wondering how it fits into the great adventures of old:

> And we shouldn't be here at all, if we'd known more about it before we started. But I suppose it's often that way. The brave things in the old tales and songs, Mr. Frodo: adventures, as I used to call them. I used to think that they were things the wonderful folk of the stories went out and looked for, because they wanted them, because they were exciting and life was a bit dull. . . . But that's not the way of it with the tales that really mattered. . . . Folk seem to have been just landed in them, usually—their paths were laid that way, as you put it. But I expect that they had lots of chances, like us, of turning back, only they didn't. . . . I wonder what sort of tale we've fallen into.[8]

A real adventure is far bigger than you or I. We get thrown in, off-balance, and need all our wits (and a good deal of luck) to find our way through and out the other side. In a real adventure, the author is the master of the story. As readers (or viewers) we are sometimes given clues as to what will happen, but never know the full story. The char-

8 J. R. R. Tolkien, *The Two Towers* (New York: Ballantine Books, 1965), 378–79.

acters in the tale, however, just have to get along as they can. They can't get out of the story; they can't climb a tall mountain to see things from a neutral perspective. They are *stuck* in the story and must keep going, not knowing what the end will be.

This quality of real adventures offers a profound insight into our own lives. We commonly ask the Lord God to reveal his full will for us and show us the path ahead. And rightly and reasonably so. But the Lord, being the Author of all authors, knows better than to pull aside the curtain and show us all that is coming. In fact, doing this would prevent us from being genuine characters in our own real adventure and would rob us of our free participation. No, we have to walk the road "in the valley of the shadow of death" and live by faith. We can be confident that God will open the door and show us the way ahead (just in the nick of time) and that we will find the resources we need along the way. But I am not the author of the story that I am in. I cannot write the script for my own adventure.

The second mark is this: a real adventure is never trivial but concerns matters of genuine importance. Adventures for very young children are plain fun; they will have a little risk thrown in, but often they (rightly) concern lighter matters. But the great adventures—for both children and adults—concern matters of real importance. The stakes are high, the losses are real, and it matters whether the characters respond in the right way. In *Treasure Island,* Jim Hawkins, still a boy, ends up with the fate of the whole crew in his hands, and he has to use his skill and intelligence many times over to help them survive and bring home the treasure. In *The Lord of the Rings*, the fate of the whole world is at stake. Gandalf reveals to Frodo the peril that surrounds him and informs him that the world's fate hinges on what happens with Frodo's ring: "The Enemy still lacks one thing to give him strength and knowledge to beat down all resistance, break the last defences, and cover all the lands in a second darkness. He lacks the One Ring."[9] Frodo is terrified and initially tries to squirm out of the quest that lies before him—thankfully he does not succeed.

Frodo's unsuccessful attempt to evade his appointed task recalls a similar figure who was given a momentous mission. The Lord appeared to Moses and spoke from the burning bush, telling Moses of his plan to deliver the people of Israel from Egypt: "Come, I will send you to Pharaoh that you may bring forth my people, the sons of Israel, out of Egypt" (Exod 3:10, RSVCE). Four times Moses tries to worm his way out of the job. First he objects that he does not have the stature for this great mission. In reply, the Lord promises his help and support, but Moses again objects: "But behold, they will not believe me or listen to my voice, for they will say, 'The LORD did not appear to you'" (Exod 4:1). The Lord then performs miracles through Moses that are to convince the people. But Moses is not persuaded: now he complains that he doesn't have the eloquence for this dangerous task. Undeterred, the Lord promises Moses that he will send Aaron to be his spokesman. Finally, Moses just asks to be

---

[9] J. R. R. Tolkien, *The Fellowship of the Ring* (New York: Ballantine Books, 1965), 76.

released: "Oh, my Lord, send, I pray, some other person" (Exod 4:13, RSVCE). But the Lord insists, and in the end, Moses takes up his role (with the help of Aaron) and the people are delivered.

This debate between Moses and the Lord is somewhat comical, but we sympathize with Moses because of the great task that is being laid upon him. He rightly recognizes that this mission is way beyond him. He doesn't have the natural eloquence or power or charisma to pull it off. The greatness of the task, beyond the powers of the one who is called, is a mark of real adventures. This, of course, is what makes them interesting.

In an essay, "The Weight of Glory," C. S. Lewis attempts to persuade us that our daily lives and interactions, seemingly so bland and dull and uneventful, are stacked with significance. He opens our eyes to see that in these daily events we are interacting with immortal souls who will become either glorious beings or hideous creatures. And we have the awesome task of influencing these destinies every day of our lives.

> All day long we are, in some degree, helping each other to one or other of these destinations. It is in the light of these overwhelming possibilities, it is with the awe and the circumspection proper to them, that we should conduct all our dealings with one another, all friendships, all loves, all play, all politics. There are no ordinary people. You have

never talked to a mere mortal.[10]

If we have eyes to see, our daily lives are filled with immensely significant interactions that have eternal consequences. In ourselves we don't have what we need to fulfill our role. We need the help and grace of God all along the way.

Here is the third mark: a real adventure includes struggle, trial, setback, plenty of discomfort, genuine perplexity, and sacrificial suffering. Arranged adventures may make us sweat a bit and push us to certain limits, but a real adventure throws us completely out of our own reckoning and involves trial and suffering beyond what we would willingly invent for ourselves. Where is the real adventure if there is no danger? Where is the meaning if there is no struggle for the good? By giving way to both envy and gluttony, Edmund places himself under the evil queen of Narnia and betrays his own siblings—and Aslan must therefore suffer shame and death to redeem Edmund (and the world) from the clutches of the evil queen. Frodo and Sam go into unimaginable darkness to take the Ring to the fire, and despite succeeding in his mission, Frodo is forever marked with the pain and grief of the burden he had to bear.

Consider the account Paul the Apostle gives of his apostolic ministry. In his Second Letter to the Corinthians, he speaks about the great trials that he and his missionary team experienced in the province of Asia. Using strong

---

10 C. S. Lewis, "The Weight of Glory," June 8, 1942, http://www.verber. com/mark/xian/weight-of-glory.pdf.

language, he acknowledges that they were so completely and utterly crushed that they gave up hope of even staying alive. But Paul recognized that this trial caused them to rely on God rather than on themselves. In the end they were delivered from death and strengthened in hope to carry on their missionary work (2 Cor 1:8–10). Even Paul was pushed beyond the limit of his own endurance. He had to find new strength in the power of God to endure and come through the trial.

As readers, we often forget how much the characters we love must suffer to win through to victory. Yet it is the challenges they endure and the trials they fight through that make them attractive and inspiring. Like so many of the characters in the great stories, we would rather stay in our quiet living rooms, safe within the walls of our own contrived adventures. But there is no gain or glory in this. It is not for this that we were made. To fulfill the true meaning of our lives, there's no way forward except through the crucible of suffering that comes with real adventure.

CHRISTIANITY: THE GREAT ADVENTURE

And now we come to the main point. The Gospel is the true narrative of our world. It is *the* great adventure: all other adventures are tributaries that flow into it (and out from it). When we finish reading our favorite story, we can place the book back on the shelf and it remains there until we wish to turn to it again. But when we finish reading the Bible and place it back on the shelf, the story continues all around us. The book is on the shelf but the story it describes continues to swirl around us and draw us in, whether we wish it to or not. We are taken up into this story, this narrative, and like the characters in a story, we can't step out of the story we are in. We are like Noah, who found himself faced with a flood he could not avoid; or Abraham, who was called to go off to a strange country; or Moses, who heard a voice from a burning bush, troubling his peaceful life; or David, who was called in from the fields and anointed as king by Samuel.

But here is the truly unexpected and astonishing truth about the story we read in the Bible: the *author* of the story steps into the world he has created and becomes the central character in the plot. The author, who had the story in mind from the beginning, whose providence has ruled over all of it, decides to enter the story and become one of the characters within it. "In the beginning was the Word. . . . All things were made through him. . . . And the Word became flesh and dwelt among us" (John 1:1–3, 14, RSVCE). The one who made everything, who created the world and all its characters *from nothing*, stepped into that world.

In fact, we come to learn that the author of this story had been preparing for his entrance into it all along, since the opening scenes. But when God the Son entered the world—a world brought into being through him (Col 1:16)—he didn't come with fanfare and trumpets announcing who he was to all the world. He came to a young virgin, and was born in a stable, and had shepherds as his first attendants. And mysteriously he came to suffer and die, knowing that he would be rejected by the very ones he came to deliver. He was invited (by the devil) to display his full power and offered dominion over all the nations of the earth (Matt 4:8–9). But he chose the path of suffering, of rejection, of apparent defeat. *And he died.* He really died and was put in the tomb.

But to the amazement of all—even the angels—he was raised again to new life. He didn't just come back to life; he was raised to a new kind of life. And instead of punishing and destroying those who put him to death—as would happen in nearly all of our created adventures—he chose to forgive them and to welcome them into friendship with himself and the Father. In a manner beyond our ability to grasp fully, he has now defeated everything that enslaved us—sin, death, and the devil. Jesus Christ, the Lamb of God, now reigns as the true king of all the world, orchestrating the spiritual battle against the devil for the salvation of the world. This is the story that we read in the Gospels, prepared for marvelously in the Old Testament.

But then at a certain point you and I entered the world. Like characters that appear in the midst of a great epic, we were born into the world and now take our place in this great narrative adventure. We can't step out of this story and fabricate one of our own. We can't leap off the page and take a break. (We can try, but it won't work.) We are in this story and need to walk down its pages, making use of all our strength, wisdom, and (most importantly) faith in God.

There is a powerful scene in *The Lord of the Rings* that shows what happens when "normal" characters realize that they've been caught up in a momentous story. Sam and Frodo are just about to enter Mordor, the final lap of the quest. While resting and chatting they suddenly see themselves anew, as caught up in one of the heroic stories that they love. Sam is speaking: "I wonder if we shall ever be put into songs or tales. We're in one, of course; but I mean: put into words, you know, told by the fireside, or read out of a great big book with red and black letters, years and years afterwards." Frodo agrees but wonders if things are going to turn out badly in their story: "We're going on a bit too fast. You and I, Sam, are still stuck in the worst places of the story, and it is all too likely that some will say at this point: 'Shut the book now, dad; we don't want to read any more.'" Sam isn't so sure—he doesn't want to give up hope: "Things done and over and made into part of the great tales are different."[11]

Frodo and Sam see themselves in a new light: as characters in the great drama of their age. They are able to place themselves in the great stories of their world and perceive that there is really only one long, connected story—and they are now caught up in the latest act of that story. Importantly, this doesn't hinder their ability to act as true and free characters. Quite the opposite: it helps them see that things are *not* as dark as they seem. They grasp their own role and the hand of providence that seems to be guiding them, and they are enabled to move ahead with greater focus and purpose.

So it is with us. The story of the Gospel can seem unreal, a story from the distant past that has little *real* relation to our day. For many, the Gospel is just a *religious* story, a kind of parable that gives us inspiring images for how to live. But it is not the real world of school and jobs and relationships and the material goods we need in order to make our way in the world. How many profess-

---

[11] Tolkien, *The Two Towers*, 379–80.

ing Christians stride out into the world and mistakenly take their cues from our wider culture, trying to forge an identity, a purpose in life, a path to walk? To encounter the living Christ means finding ourselves transported into *his* story and to take our place in the costly adventure of discipleship that he has marked out for each of us. Being a Christian is not just a matter of turning to God and finding help and consolation in the challenging circumstances of life. To become a follower of Jesus means leaving behind the identities we have created for ourselves and the adventures that we have dreamed up, and entering onto the path marked out by the call of God.

This is what Paul means when he says, "It is no longer I who live, but Christ who lives in me. And the life I now live in the flesh I live by faith in the Son of God, who loved me and gave himself for me" (Gal 2:20, ESV). Discipleship redefines our lives from top to bottom. We realize that we have been inserted into a new "narrative," a profound "adventure" not of our own making. Before we were looking at the Christian life as a spectator, from the sidelines. Now we have been thrown in and are playing on the field.

The story of Eustace Scrubb wonderfully illustrates this transition from spectator to actor. In *The Voyage of the Dawn Treader*, C. S. Lewis presents Eustace as a skeptical, snotty boy who delights in mocking the silly, fanciful stories told about the land of Narnia by his cousins, Lucy and Edmund Pevensie. One day, the three are standing in a room examining a picture of a boat on the high seas. Suddenly the picture comes to life, the wind and spray begin to blow into the room, and all three children are hurled through the picture frame into the world of Narnia.

> Eustace rushed towards the picture. . . . And by this time either they had grown much smaller or the picture had grown much bigger. Eustace jumped to try to pull it off the wall and found himself standing on the frame; in front of him was not glass but real sea, and wind and waves rushing up to the frame as they might to a rock. He lost his head and clutched at the other two who had jumped up beside him. There was a second of struggling and shouting, and just as they thought they had got their balance a great blue roller surged up round them, swept them off their feet, and drew them down into the sea.[12]

Something like this happens when we encounter Christ and the power of the Holy Spirit. What seemed like a "still" picture that we could safely examine suddenly comes to life and draws us in. We awaken to the *real* world that we are in and this transforms how we think about everything in our lives.

* * * * *

The aim of this first chapter is to offer an imaginative vision for what it means to be disciples of Jesus Christ. We began by considering our natural love for adventure and then peered more deeply into what real adventures

---

[12] C. S. Lewis, *The Voyage of the Dawn Treader* (New York: HarperCollins, 1980), 9–10.

are like. My intention was to help us see that the story recounted in the Gospels—and throughout the Bible—is the privileged and inspired record of the true story of our world. This is the great adventure that encompasses all of us, whether we like it or not. Being a Christian is not just a set of beliefs or a moral code or a set of practices— though it is certainly all of these things. At the core of being a Christian is becoming a disciple of Jesus Christ. A key part of discipleship is setting out, like Abraham and the first Apostles, on a path of adventure that will cost us our whole lives.

The chapters that follow unfold and develop this basic theme. They seek to answer the following questions: What is entailed in becoming a disciple? What is the cost of discipleship and why does God ask for this cost? Who is this Jesus that we are following? What roles do faith, hope, and love play in the outworking of the adventure of our lives? And what is the goal? Where is all this going?

* *Portrait* *
THE VIRGIN MARY

No one has been caught up into the great adventure of the Gospel more fully and profoundly than Mary of Nazareth, the Mother of God. Yes, she received all the grace needed to fulfill her role in God's plan, but this does not mean that she was forewarned in detail about what God would ask and was able to practice her part ahead of time, like an actress rehearsing her lines. The angel Gabriel appears without forewarning, "out of the blue," and when he greets Mary, she is genuinely (and greatly) perplexed, wondering in her thoughts what this greeting might mean (Luke 1:29). Gabriel then tells of God's plan, that she is to bear a son, the Messiah, the son of David. Mary's response comes in the form of a question: "How will this be?" It will occur through the power of the Spirit, explains Gabriel: "The Holy Spirit will come upon you, and the power of the Most High will overshadow you" (Luke 1:35).

The drama here is intense. What will Mary do? How will she respond to this unexpected interruption into her life? Proving herself to be the model disciple, Mary replies, "Behold, I am the handmaid of the Lord; let it be to me according to your word" (Luke 1:38, RSVCE). There was no precedent for this. No woman before had ever been with child through the Holy Spirit and borne the very Son of God. The annunciation of the angel Gabriel to Mary displays in marvelous contours the unexpected, momentous quality of a real adventure. And this was to be a *costly* adventure for Mary: she is promised that a sword will also pierce through her own heart (Luke 2:35). In Mary's free response to the initiative of God, "Let it be done to me according to your word," we come face to face with the core of what it means to be a disciple of Jesus.

·❖·

CHAPTER TWO

A VENTURESOME FAITH

In this consists the excellence and nobleness of
faith; this is the very reason why faith is singled
out from other graces . . . because its presence implies that we have the heart to make a venture.

—John Henry Newman[1]

IN his inaugural homily, just after his election as pope,
St. John Paul II exhorted the faithful, "Do not be afraid!"
This phrase became a hallmark of his papacy. Here are his
opening words at greater length:

Brothers and sisters, do not be afraid to welcome
Christ and accept his power. . . . Do not be afraid.
Open wide the doors for Christ. To his saving
power open the boundaries of states, economic

---

[1] John Henry Newman, "The Ventures of Faith," *Parochial and Plain
Sermons* (San Francisco: Ignatius Press, 1987), 914.

29

and political systems, the vast fields of culture, civilization and development. Do not be afraid.[2]

Later in his pontificate, as the new millennium unfolded, John Paul made use of a different phrase to communicate the same venturesome spirit. He called the faithful to "put out into the deep" (in Latin, *duc in altum*).[3] The phrase comes from the Gospel of Luke (5:4). Jesus calls Peter to put his nets out into the deep for a catch of fish. Peter is doubtful—he has fished all night and caught nothing— but obeys. The result is a haul of fish so great that the nets almost burst. By this phrase, *duc in altum*, John Paul is calling us to leave safe waters, to set aside small expectations, and to let down our nets with boldness for a great catch.

AN AGE OF FEAR, INSECURITY, AND *ACEDIA*

The time we live in has been called an age of doubt, insecurity, and fear. In the same year that the Pope called us to "put out into the deep," R. R. Reno, then a professor at Creighton University, offered an analysis of the dominant spirit or mood animating young people at the start of the new millennium: "The outlook of modernity has shifted from ambition and confidence to fear and anxiety. The spirit of the age is no longer self-expressive; it is

[2] Pope John Paul II, *Homily of His Holiness John Paul II for the Inauguration of His Pontificate* (October 22, 1978), available from http://www.vatican.va.
[3] Pope John Paul II, Apostolic Letter *Novo Millennio Ineunte* (January 6, 2001), §15, available from http://www.vatican.va.

self-protective."[4] In Reno's estimation, young people today are not particularly rebellious, but they are not ambitious or venturesome either. Rather, they have become detached and independent, seeking safe spaces to protect themselves in a relativistic world that offers little ground on which to stand and build.

Others have identified *acedia*, or spiritual sloth, as the characteristic vice of our age, especially among the young.[5] Sloth is an inclination to idleness, to aimlessness, to apathy in action. When it infects the soul deeply, it leads to discouragement and despair. Taught to believe that all truth is relative and therefore changeable, and often faced with little hope for satisfying and meaningful work, young people retreat to enclaves of entertainment where the digital age has equipped them with endless—usually mindless—distraction.

In such a climate, the words of John Paul, "do not be afraid" and "put out into the deep," have tremendous relevance. They are needed now more than ever. We have need of adventures—and venturesome spirits—that pull us out of our doldrums and propel us to set out on a pilgrim's journey. But they also remind us of a crucial truth: we don't have to concoct or artificially arrange for these adventures. Doing this would only be one more form of distraction, just another contrived escape from a meaningless world. The glad truth is that we have already landed in a great

[4] R. R. Reno, "American Satyricon," *First Things* (October 2001), https://www.firstthings.com/article/2001/10/american-satyricon.

[5] See, for example, R. J. Snell, *Acedia and Its Discontents: Metaphysical Boredom in an Empire of Desire* (2015), and Jean-Charles Nault, *The Noonday Devil: Acedia, the Unnamed Evil of Our Times* (2015).

and true adventure that is full of meaning, significance, uncertainty, and even danger. This adventure is called discipleship to Jesus Christ—and it is available to everyone.

In this chapter I hope to offer a sketch of the kind of spirit needed to engage and embrace the adventurous life that is ours through the Gospel, and to contrast this spirit with its competitors and counterfeits. Along the way I will call upon the teaching of the Catechism and the wise insights of Blessed John Henry Newman to help us grasp what a venturesome faith looks like.

FAITH THAT ENTRUSTS AND ACTS

The core meaning of faith is belief in God and all that he has revealed: "Faith is the theological virtue by which we believe in God and believe all that he has said and revealed to us, and that Holy Church proposes for our belief, because he is truth itself" (CCC 1814). But faith also includes the full commitment of our lives, what the Catechism calls the commitment of our entire selves to God (1814). The implication is that true faith, as it grows and matures in us, cannot remain simply within our minds as a belief or conviction; it manifests itself in personal commitment as we entrust ourselves completely to God. "Faith is first of all a personal adherence of man to God. . . . It is right and just to entrust oneself wholly to God and to believe absolutely what he says" (150). Or as the Catechism says elsewhere, "To believe is to say 'Amen' to God's words, promises and commandments; to entrust oneself completely to him who is the 'Amen' of infinite love and perfect faithfulness" (1064).

This is just how the book of Hebrews illustrates what

faith is. After defining faith as "the substance of things hoped for, the evidence of things not seen" (Heb 11:1), Hebrews illustrates what faith is by showing *faith in action*. "By faith," Abel, Enoch, Noah, Abraham, Moses, and many others acted upon God's word. They "lived by faith" and did not shrink back from acting upon the word of God that came to each of them. This is the kind of faith we need in order to embrace the costly adventure of discipleship: a faith that believes God and his word, that enables us to commit ourselves completely to God, and that empowers us to act freely upon God's word. This is venturesome faith.

THE VENTURES OF FAITH ACCORDING TO JOHN HENRY NEWMAN

In a sermon given in 1836, John Henry Newman speaks forcefully about the "ventures of faith" that are required of the Christian. He begins the sermon by establishing the need for making such ventures: "Here then a great lesson is impressed upon us, that our duty as Christians lies in this, in making ventures for eternal life without the absolute certainty of success."[6] Newman then offers his thesis on what it means to make a venture of faith:

This, indeed, is the very meaning of the word "venture"; for that is a strange venture which has nothing in it of fear, risk, danger, anxiety, uncertainty. Yes, so it is; and in this consists the excellence and nobleness of faith; this is the very

---

[6] Newman, "The Ventures of Faith," 914.

reason why faith is singled out from other graces
. . . because its presence implies that we have the
heart to make a venture.[7]

Ranging across the Scriptures, Newman shows how these
ventures of faith are expressed throughout the history of
God's people: from Abraham to the Apostles and in the
Letter to the Hebrews. As a contrast, he points to the *failure* of the rich young man of the Gospel to make a venture
of faith: he walked away sad because he lacked the faith
needed to respond to Christ's invitation.

Newman does not refer to the parable of the talents in
the Gospel of Matthew (25:14–30), but it illustrates his
point with clarity. Three servants are each given a set of
resources of varying amounts. The first and second trade
with what they received and bring a return to their master.
The third, afraid to lose what he had, buries his talent
and returns it with no interest, with nothing gained. Jesus
denounces the third servant for being wicked and sloth-
ful—he gave way to fear and did not "venture" to invest
the resources he was given. This can appear as a harsh
handling of the fearful servant, but Christ offers the parable to show how important it is that we *act* upon the
faith we have received and bring a return to the Lord. For
Newman, "If then faith be the essence of a Christian life
. . . it follows that our duty lies in risking upon Christ's
word what we have, for what we have not." And here he
qualifies this claim with a set of statements that define
the contours of venturesome faith. We are to act in faith,

---

[7] Newman, "The Ventures of Faith," 914.

doing so in a noble, generous way, not indeed rashly or lightly, still without knowing accurately what we are doing, not knowing either what we give up, nor again what we shall gain; uncertain about our reward, uncertain about our extent of sacrifice, in all respects leaning, waiting upon him, trusting in him to fulfill his promise, trusting in him to enable us to fulfill our own vows.[8]

There is nothing safe, secure, or predictable about the kind of faith Newman describes here. On the one hand, this active, venturing faith is noble and generous: it is not fearful or constrained. On the other hand, it should not be equated with being rash or frivolous. It is grounded in the faithfulness and providence of God.

At this point it is crucial to distinguish a venturesome faith from its imposters and counterfeits. Some people have a natural disposition to be adventurous; they become easily bored with routine and like to take risks. Often they push themselves to extremes, risking health and life in the pursuit of danger or new experiences. This is *not* the venturesome faith Newman is pointing to. Other people are naturally cautious; they weigh things carefully and rarely take steps that are genuinely risky. They are risk-averse. Natural dispositions of both kinds can be of great service to us or can become a significant hindrance, but they should not be confused with godly virtue. The virtuous person is one who knows when to take a risk and when to step back in caution. Whether we are naturally risk-takers

---

[8] Newman, "The Ventures of Faith," 916.

or naturally risk-averse, we are all called to invest our lives in the kingdom of God with a venturesome faith.

We can risk our lives because of the light and certainty that our faith gives us. By faith we trust in Christ absolutely, rely upon his word, and can risk our lives on the strength of his word. By faith we also know that God watches over our lives and that he will work all things to the good for those who love him. We do *not* know, as Newman reminds us, how the details of our lives will work out. We set out on a course and put our whole lives at Christ's service, and we trust him to lead us to a good end. As is true with any good story or adventure, we as the characters in the story cannot see what will happen in the pages ahead. We have to take things step by step, page by page, trusting in God and following the path laid out before us. It is our faith, in combination with hope and love, that enables us to venture our lives with confidence in God.

Newman concludes the sermon with a challenge. He wonders aloud whether most Christians really have the heart to make a venture of faith.

This is the question, What have we ventured? . . . I really fear that most men called Christians, whatever they may profess, whatever they may think they feel, whatever warmth and illumination and love they may claim as their own, yet would go on almost as they do, neither much better nor much worse, if they believed Christianity to be a fable. . . . They venture nothing, they risk, they sacrifice, they abandon nothing on the faith of Christ's word.[9]

Newman is challenging the Christians of his day, and by extension challenging all of us, to examine ourselves. Are we living a comfortable, worldly form of Christianity or are we really risking our lives for the sake of Christ? Would our lives really look different if we did not believe in Christ? Does faith in Christ genuinely shape our decisions and choices? The closing lines of the sermon renew the challenge: "I repeat it; what are our ventures and risks upon the truth of his word?"[10] Citing Jesus's words in Matthew 19:29–30, Newman ends by consoling his listeners with the promise that those who have left everything for the sake of the kingdom of heaven will receive a hundredfold in this life and inherit eternal life.

FOUR TYPES OF RESPONSES

In the spirit of examining our lives as recommended by Newman, I would like to present four discrete *types* of responses to the Gospel. Each of these responses has marked my own life at one time or another, but I have also seen them unfold in the lives of many young people. Each one describes a certain vision for life, but in fact each points to a type of character. The danger of using "types" of course is that they generalize and so can fail to grasp the special features of an individual life. But despite this limitation they can provide a helpful lens to examine our

---

[9] Newman, "The Ventures of Faith," 917–18.
[10] Newman, "The Ventures of Faith," 921.

own lives and consider whether we have the venturesome faith that enables us freely to "put out into the deep." To be clear, in my descriptions I am assuming that all four types of people have heard the Gospel and responded in some fashion. The seed has been sown and has sprung up in their lives. But as in the parable of the sower, the soil and environment around the seedling make an enormous difference for how the seed grows and bears fruit.

The Ideal Castle. The first type is marked by a vision of life that I call "the ideal castle." People of this type have a vision of the kind of "castle" they want to build. All the labors, all the hours of study in school, all the low-paying jobs, all the hours spent in the gym, are aimed at a kind of ideal life they want to attain. This ideal vision is what really motivates them, what supplies the energy needed to make sacrifices. Christian Smith has done extensive sociological studies on youth and emerging adults today. One of his consistent findings is that a surprisingly large number of young people are *not* fired by high ideals for changing the world, but are aiming at a comfortable path in which they possess the time and the gadgets to carry on a modern consumer lifestyle.[11]

Many of the things in this "ideal castle" may be fine and good—but this isn't the point exactly. Those who seek this vision of the good life are fundamentally self-focused: everything is ordered to gaining this castle for themselves.

---

[11] See Christian Smith and Kari Christoffersen, *Lost in Transition: The Dark Side of Emerging Adulthood* (Oxford: Oxford University Press, 2011), especially Chapter Two, "Captive to Consumerism."

They are tempted to treat friends, family, and activities as *means* to an end. They often don't know deep friendship or the great freedom that comes from giving things away without thought of return. And they are *earthbound*, caught up in gaining things in this world, reluctant to reconcile themselves to the extreme shortness of life, the insecurity of things in this world, and the emptiness of gaining them.

Jesus promises his disciples something like a castle of his own making. He says that he has gone ahead of us to prepare "rooms" or "mansions" for us (John 14:2). But these will be quite different from the mansions we build here. In eternal life God himself is the fundamental reward, and our inheritance is the holy city where we will dwell without tears in the presence of God. In this life we are called to sacrifice and to live as aliens and exiles, waiting for a kingdom that cannot be bought at any earthly price.

What is Christ's counsel for those of us who want to follow Christ but who seek an earthly castle as well? "No servant can serve two masters. . . .You cannot serve God and money" (Luke 16:13, ESV). And "if anyone would come after me, let him deny himself and take up his cross and follow me" (Matt 16:24, ESV).

The Obstacle Course. The second type is characterized by people who relate to life—including spiritual life—like an obstacle course. They are often very faithful and reliable people, concerned with doing well and clearing all the hurdles that life throws up. In fact, clearing the next hurdle becomes the goal of life. They recognize that life is full of challenges and want to make sure that they are always prepared, always equipped, always ready to clear the next hurdle.

When we look a bit deeper, we see that "obstacle-course" people are fundamentally anxious about the future and about possible failure. In a sense, it is failure that motivates them. They desperately want to avoid failing, and so look at life as a long set of obstacles to be cleared and overcome. As a result, they seldom *enjoy* anything—they are always worried about the next hurdle down the track. And surprisingly, they are often highly cautious, because the greatest motivation is fear, not glory or wonder or excellence. Aimed at clearing the next obstacle in the path, they rarely venture anything.

The words of Jesus from the Sermon on the Mount speak directly to this condition. He charges us not to be anxious about our lives—what we shall eat or drink or wear. Instead he calls us to seek first his kingdom and his justice. As we do this, all these other things we worry about will be ours as well (Matt 6:25–33). The Apostle Peter also addresses those caught up in fear and anxiety, telling them to cast all their anxieties and worries on God because God cares for them (1 Pet 5:7).

The Sluggard. The third type of person is marked by indolence, laziness, and lack of ambition in life. The Book of Proverbs calls this person a "sluggard" and offers poignant, humorous descriptions of his behavior:

How long will you lie there, O sluggard? When will you arise from your sleep? (Prov 6:9, ESV)

> The desire of the sluggard kills him, for his
> hands refuse to labor. (Prov 21:25, ESV)

> As a door turns on its hinges, so does a sluggard
> on his bed. (Prov 26:14, ESV)

There is probably some part of each of us that painfully resembles these descriptions.

But the problem we face today is much graver than just laziness. There is a spiritual sloth, *acedia*, which has become something of an epidemic in our day. It has been rightly analyzed, I think, as grounded in a lack of *hope*. Many young people lack hope for life; they lack ambition to do anything but "hang out and have a good time." When there's nowhere to go and no real reason to go there, well . . . let's just cool out and have fun. This is a kind of sickness, but it's also a spirit and a mood that needs to be shaken off or else it slowly kills. In fact, our lives are deeply meaningful. There is much at stake. A profound lie exists at heart of this cultural *acedia* that robs people of their God-given dignity and the significance of their lives.

The "sluggard" needs to be roused by the truth of the Gospel: to come to know that he or she really matters to the living God. "My life" is something worth fighting for, laboring for, sacrificing for. At least the Lord Jesus thought so—he paid a huge price so that we might live. And in the end, it is love that conquers the sickness of *acedia*. We need the Holy Spirit to fill us with zeal for the love of God and one another in order to overcome the sick despair of the sluggard.

What is the word of the Lord for those of us who find

ourselves in this place of sadness and despair? The Psalms speak to this and call us to hope: "Why are you cast down, O my soul, and why are you disquieted within me? Hope in God; for I shall again praise him, my help and my God" (Ps 42:5–6, RSVCE). Paul's famous words in Romans chapter eight also reveal the antidote to this sickness: the effective activity of the Holy Spirit in the heart of the believer. He assures us that all those led by the Spirit of God are indeed sons and daughters of God. God did not give us a spirit of slavery that grovels in fear, but rather a spirit of "sonship" that leads us to cry out, "Abba, Father." We can have hope because we are *children of God*, who are heirs of God's blessings (Rom 8:14–17).

Venturesome Faith. Let's return to Cardinal Newman's exhortation to live for Christ with a venturesome faith. What does this entail and how does it contrast with the types described above? People who have a venturesome faith are bold without being rash. They set their eyes on great things (this is the virtue of magnanimity). They are motivated not by fear of failure but by the possibility of success in Christ and are willing to risk and to venture to gain it. They know that they can do nothing by them-selves, but enlivened by God's life and power they know (with Paul) that they can do all things through the one who strengthens them (Phil 4:13).

They know that their lives are not centered here in this life, and so they can venture everything and not fear to lose it. Their treasure is in heaven, and so they can live freely on earth and be bold for the sake of the kingdom. Even when they encounter severe obstacles or hard suffering, they look to the Lord for strength and finds help in time of need (Heb 4:16). People with a venturesome faith are characterized by joy, not by anxiety. They can embrace others as true friends, especially those who serve together in the common cause for Christ. They can enjoy the good things in life that come their way because they are not possessed by them; they know that their true treasure in is heaven. These are not narrow individuals, but expansive ones, bearing fruit in every season (Ps 1:3).

These are the ones who, when Christ returns and asks for an account, will be able to say, "Master, you delivered to me five talents; here I have made five talents more," and they will enter into the joy of their master (Matt 25:20–21, RSVCE). Like Paul, they have learned to trust in God completely; they know that their competence comes from God and not from themselves (2 Cor 3:4–5). And with Paul, they are marked by a readiness to let go of what lies in the past and to press ahead until the Lord calls them home (Phil 3:13–14). This is the heritage of those who respond to the call of Jesus with venturesome faith.

THE JOY OF DISCIPLESHIP

To remind us: in Christ, our lives are caught up in *a great and costly adventure*, not of our making or contrivance. Somehow, even though we are apparently small and unimportant, our lives are unbelievably, unreasonably important to the author of this story.

To conclude, I wish to point to the quality of "joy" that accompanies our full-hearted response to the Gospel. In his Apostolic Exhortation, *Evangelii Gaudium* (2015), Pope Francis calls the people of God to embrace the joy that belongs to disciples of Christ: "The joy of the Gospel fills the hearts and lives of all who encounter Jesus. Those who accept his offer of salvation are set free from sin, sorrow, inner emptiness and loneliness. With Christ joy is constantly born anew."[12]

The same accent on joy is found in Jesus's parable of the treasure hidden in the field: "The kingdom of heaven is like treasure hidden in a field, which a man found and covered up. Then in his joy he goes and sells all that he has and buys that field" (Matt 13:44, ESV). This two-sentence parable is packed with insight about what discipleship is. Perhaps the man in the parable was actively seeking for treasure, but more likely he stumbled across this treasure accidentally. Realizing what he has found, he quickly covers it up before anyone sees what he has discovered, and runs off to purchase the field so that he has rights to the treasure. Notice that he does so "in his joy." He is filled with joy at the prospect of selling everything he has in order to buy the field and obtain so great a treasure. In the next chapter we will pursue this question of selling everything for the kingdom of God. Here I want to draw our attention to the joy that accompanies the discovery of the kingdom of God. With joy we exchange everything we possess for a treasure that is far greater than we could ever obtain on our own.

If our hearts are set on some other "ideal castle," then we will be tempted to ignore the treasure hidden in the

---

[12] Pope Francis, The Joy of the Gospel *Evangelii Gaudium* (November 24, 2013), § 1, available from http://www.vatican.va (hereafter cited in text as EG).

field because we are seeking a different treasure. If we live in fear and anxiety, afraid of failure and seeking only to clear the next hurdle, then we may have found the treasure but we will lack the faith and confidence to sell everything in order to really make it ours. If we are captive to sluggishness and even despair, we may have stumbled across the treasure of the kingdom of God but we will lack the hope and zeal to act and so make it our own. But when we allow the Lord God to capture our hearts and set out with adventurous faith to pursue the path set before us, then the treasure will be ours, along with the joy of possessing it—the joy of knowing God and being joined to his people.

* *Portrait* *
ABRAHAM

Abraham is best known for being the father of faith: he is the model and exemplar of what it means to hear the word of God and obey it, even when not knowing where it will lead. Consider the opening words of Genesis chapter twelve: "Now the LORD said to Abram, 'Go from your country and your kindred and your father's house to the land that I will show you. . . .' So Abram went, as the LORD had told him" (Gen 12:1, 4, RSVCE). The biblical account simply says that Abraham "went as the LORD told him." That's it—he set out to a land he did not know and staked his whole life on God's word to him. The Letter to the Hebrews comments on these very verses: "By faith Abraham obeyed when he was called to go out to a place which he was to receive as an inheritance; and he went out, not knowing where he was to go" (Heb 11:8, RSVCE). We are not told whether Abraham had inward doubts or had arguments with his wider family about this radical departure. He just "went as the LORD told him."

This, however, was not a one-time act of venturesome faith. Throughout his life Abraham continued to trust God and follow his leading. The culminating test was the command to take his only son Isaac, the one God himself had given miraculously, and sacrifice him back to God on the mountain. Again, Abraham just "went" to do as God had directed him. We know the story well: as Abraham is about to slay Isaac upon the altar, the angel of the Lord intervenes and a ram is offered instead. The Lord God then speaks in powerful words about the faithfulness of

Abraham: because Abraham trusted God he will be the chosen vehicle and a blessing for all the nations:

> By myself I have sworn, says the LORD: Because you have done this, and have not withheld your son, your only son, I will indeed bless you . . . and by your offspring shall all the nations of the earth gain blessing for themselves, because you have obeyed my voice. (Gen 22:16–18, NRSVCE)

Abraham models for us the venturesome faith that we are called to embrace and put into practice. By faith he set out upon an adventure that, through Christ, brought the blessing of God upon all the nations.

CHAPTER THREE

A Costly Discipleship

> Such grace is costly because it calls us to follow, and it is grace because it calls us to follow Jesus Christ. It is costly because it costs a man his life, and it is grace because it gives a man the only true life. . . . Above all, it is costly because it cost God the life of his Son.
>
> —Dietrich Bonhoeffer[1]

In this chapter we will investigate the *costly* side of the adventure of discipleship. Adventures worth their salt invariably cost the main characters a great deal—sometimes the loss of their lives. The sending of the Son by the Father into the world cost the innocent life of the Son—and by that offering the world was redeemed. In the next chapter we will explore in greater detail the costly work that Christ Jesus accomplished for our salvation. Here, we

1 Dietrich Bonhoeffer, *The Cost of Discipleship*, rev. ed. (New York: MacMillan, 1979), 47.

will attempt to look squarely at the cost of discipleship to Jesus Christ—and not flinch! What are we to make of these hard "discipleship sayings" of our Lord? Are they intended just for rhetorical effect? Or perhaps these sayings apply only to especially holy people, allowing the rest of us to slide past them and walk a much easier road?

Every age seems to produce its own version of "decaffeinated" Christianity. Through various stratagems we find ways to evade Jesus's challenging words. We domesticate his demands, seeking to make them more palatable and reduce their cost. In pre-World War II Germany, the Lutheran pastor Dietrich Bonhoeffer identified what he called the doctrine of "cheap grace." Here is his account: "Cheap grace is the deadly enemy of our Church. We are fighting today for costly grace. . . . The essence of grace, we suppose, is that the account has been paid in advance; and, because it has been paid, everything can be had for nothing."[2] Bonhoeffer vigorously resisted this version of "cheap grace," recognizing in it a profound weakness that would cause the churches to fail in the hard times that were coming upon them. He raised his voice to remind Christians that although the grace of God in Christ is entirely a free gift, yet paradoxically it costs us our whole lives. The gift is free and the response costs everything. In place of "cheap grace," Bonhoeffer urged a return to a costly discipleship:

> Christianity without the living Christ is inevitably Christianity without discipleship, and Chris-

---

[2] Bonhoeffer, *The Cost of Discipleship*, 45.

tianity without discipleship is always Christianity without Christ. It remains an abstract idea, a myth which has a place for the Fatherhood of God, but omits Christ as the living Son. And a Christianity of that kind is nothing more or less than the end of discipleship.[3]

These were not mere words for Bonhoeffer. Counselled to remain in the United States for his own safety, Bonhoeffer put himself in danger by returning to Nazi Germany because he was convinced that he was called to stand with his people under trial. In a few short years, he was arrested and imprisoned for his resistance to the regime. Just days before the war ended, he was executed. He paid the ultimate price in his commitment to follow Christ on the road of costly discipleship.

THE DISCIPLESHIP SAYINGS OF JESUS

In this section we will consider what Jesus says about the cost of entering the kingdom of God. But first we have to handle two objections. The first runs something like this: *I thought Christianity was all about love. Why all this talk about cost and suffering?* The story of the Gospel *is* all about love: the love of God for his creation and the creatures made in his image and likeness. In love, God sent his Son into the world to redeem the world (John 3:17); in love, Christ offered up his innocent life for the guilty. And God has poured his love into our hearts through the Holy Spirit (Rom 5:5). We are called to love God and one

---

[3] Bonhoeffer, *The Cost of Discipleship*, 63–64.

another as the first and greatest commandments (Mark 12:28–31). But the love God showed us was a *costly* love. When was there a love story worth reading that did not involve danger and sacrifice for the lovers? We know that love is always costly and that lovers are glad to be able to express love by paying a high price. The cost of discipleship is nothing other than our sharing in the costly love that God has shown to us: it is our privilege to share in this cost. It is also the path that God has given us so that we may walk in imitation of his Son.

A second objection points to Christ's ministry of mercy and healing in the Gospels and asks: *Didn't Christ just heal people freely, in many cases without calling them to personal discipleship? Isn't the heart of the Gospel meeting people's needs, freely and without cost? This is what Jesus did.* Jesus certainly lavished mercy on multitudes, feeding the hungry with bread, healing all kinds of diseases, delivering many from the power of evil spirits, and giving hope to the poor and downtrodden. The Church, which is the body of Christ, continues this work of mercy. Pope Francis highlighted this aspect of mission by calling the Church a field-hospital where many can find mercy, grace, and healing.[4]

But while Christ freely showed mercy to all, *at the same time* he called people to enter the kingdom of God and begin to live its way of life. The Sermon on the Mount is a teaching given to the "disciples" of Jesus (beginning in Matt 5:1), but it's clear that the crowds were invited to

---

[4] Address of Pope Francis to the Parish Priests of the Diocese of Rome (March 6, 2014), available from http://www.vatican.va.

listen and respond (Matt 7:28–29). Jesus worked closely with a small number of followers and "discipled" them, but his strategy was to reach the multitudes through his disciples and call those multitudes also to a life of discipleship. His final charge to the Apostles is to "make disciples of all nations" (Matt 28:19–20). The gift of the Spirit is freely poured out on all people so that everyone—at the right time—can receive the call to discipleship and be equipped to respond.

As a prelude to considering the discipleship sayings of Jesus, let's return briefly to the two short parables where Jesus speaks of the kingdom as a treasure and a pearl of great price. Here they are in full:

> The kingdom of heaven is like treasure hidden in a field, which a man found and covered up. Then in his joy he goes and sells all that he has and buys that field. Again, the kingdom of heaven is like a merchant in search of fine pearls, who, on finding one pearl of great value, went and sold all that he had and bought it. (Matt 13:44–46, ESV)

The two parables share a common theme. In each one we have a man who discovers something of inestimable value. The first man presumably stumbles upon this treasure, the second one scours the earth seeking it. But when they find this treasure, they sell everything they have to obtain it. The point is that the kingdom of God is a treasure beyond imagining, but to obtain it we need to "sell" everything we have. It demands the full offering of our lives. There is a great cost.

The discipleship sayings of Jesus apply this truth and make it personal. The first appears in Matthew:

> And a scribe came up and said to him, "Teacher, I will follow you wherever you go." And Jesus said to him, "Foxes have holes, and birds of the air have nests; but the Son of man has nowhere to lay his head." Another of the disciples said to him, "Lord, let me first go and bury my father." But Jesus said to him, "Follow me, and leave the dead to bury their own dead." (Matt 8:19–22, RSVCE)

Today Jesus would be faulted for his marketing strategy. This is not the way to persuade people to follow him. A scribe—a teacher of the Jewish law—approaches and commits himself to follow Jesus wherever he will go. In response, Jesus warns him that the path will not be easy or comfortable. Another disciple asks for a season to care for his father. Jesus appears to rebuff this request and call him to follow straightaway. In other words, Jesus sets a very high bar for what it means to be his follower.

A second discipleship saying appears in the Gospel of Mark:

> And summoning the crowd along with his disciples, he said to them: "If anyone wants to follow after me, let him deny himself and take up his cross and follow me. For whoever wants to save his life will lose it, but whoever loses his life for my sake and the gospel's will save it. For how is it

profitable for a man to gain the whole world and forfeit his life?" (Mark 8:34–36)

Notice that Jesus speaks these words to the whole multitude and to his disciples—this is a message for "anyone" who would seek to be his follower. He calls his followers to deny claim to their own lives, to pick up the cross of crucifixion, and to follow after him. The context is crucial: Jesus has just announced that he is going up to Jerusalem where he will be rejected and killed, and he rebukes Peter for attempting to turn him aside from this course. Now, he could have said: "I am going up to Jerusalem to die for you and your sins, and when I rise from the dead, I will return and give you all a life of freedom, peace, ease, and happiness." But this is not what he said. He invited those who would follow him to lay aside a claim to their own lives, to pick up a cross that leads to death, and to follow him on the road.

If this were not clear enough, Jesus expands on what he means. If we try to save our lives on our own, we will lose them—we cannot redeem ourselves. But if we lose our lives for Jesus and the Gospel, then we will "save" them in the end. The way of the cross presents a deep paradox: the path of discipleship means laying down our lives; only in this way will we "find" them.

A third saying from the Gospel of John confirms the cost at the core of discipleship. Jesus is approaching the hour of his death, and he speaks about that death in terms of a seed:

Truly, truly, I say to you, unless a grain of wheat falls into the earth and dies, it remains alone; but if it dies, it bears much fruit. Whoever loves his life loses it, and whoever hates his life in this world will keep it for eternal life. If anyone serves me, he must follow me; and where I am, there will my servant be also. (John 12:24–26, ESV)

This is preeminently true of Jesus himself. He is the seed who dies that others might live. But he applies this to his followers: if we love our lives and seek to preserve them, we will lose them. If we "hate" our lives—this is equivalent to "denying ourselves"—then we will keep them for eternal life. The crucial step is to follow Jesus and to be where he is.

STEPS ON THE ROAD TO DISCIPLESHIP

All this is very bracing, but really, how does it apply to us? In first-century Palestine, it was actually possible to "follow after" Jesus on the road, to adopt his way of life, to listen to his teaching day after day, and even to take up a Roman cross and be crucified with him. But none of this applies to us in a literal sense today. So what does it all mean?

It is worth observing that none of Jesus's disciples *actually* picked up their own crosses and followed him to Golgotha. We are told that Simon of Cyrene carried Jesus's Cross part of the way, but he was not even a disciple at the time, and it was not *his* cross in any case (and he was never nailed to it). Jesus made use of the image of walking the road of crucifixion to reveal what it means for all disciples of all times to follow him. To explore what this might mean for us today, I will break down the road to discipleship into three steps or stages. These stages of discipleship appear in the biblical stories and they continue to be typical stages for disciples today. First, there is a personal encounter with Jesus; second, there must be a clear decision to follow Jesus with determination; third, there will be one or more crossroads where the temptation to turn back must be rejected if we are to continue as Jesus's disciples.

Personal Encounter. In the Gospels, all who become true followers of Jesus have a personal encounter with him that is at the root of their decision to follow him. Think of Peter and Andrew, James and John, Matthew and Mary Magdalene: they listened to his teaching, they saw him heal the sick, and they heard him call them by name: "Come, follow me." The same is true for the saints down the ages. The same is true for us today. This encounter can be dramatic and powerful; it can also occur quietly through a still, small voice. In whatever manner this encounter happens, the conviction of meeting the person of Christ and hearing his call opens up the path of discipleship. To say this differently, we don't disciple ourselves; we don't take the initiative and seek to follow Christ. We respond to a call that comes through a personal encounter with the living Christ through the Spirit. Even when we are seeking him (like the rich young man in the Gospel), we come to see that it is already his grace that is at work, prompting us and drawing us to himself.

Pope Benedict repeatedly underlines the importance of an encounter with the person of Jesus. In the opening paragraph of *Deus Caritas Est*, he writes: "Being Christian is not the result of an ethical choice or a lofty idea, but the encounter with an event, a person, which gives life a new horizon and a decisive direction."[5] In *Sacramentum Caritatis*, he says that "what the world needs is God's love; it needs to encounter Christ and to believe in him."[6] Pope Francis quotes Benedict on the centrality of an encounter with Christ and adds his own strong encouragement:

> I invite all Christians, everywhere, at this very moment, to a renewed personal encounter with Jesus Christ, or at least an openness to letting him encounter them; I ask all of you to do this unfailingly each day. . . . The Lord does not disappoint those who take this risk; whenever we take a step towards Jesus, we come to realize that he is already there, waiting for us with open arms. (EG 3)

Archbishop Allen Vigneron speaks of this pivotal encounter in terms of a love affair: "The new evangelization is not a membership drive, nor is it an effort to shore up a code of conduct. Rather, it is a love affair. All are invited to encounter Jesus and let their hearts be captured by him."[7] In short, a personal encounter with the living Christ is the gateway to discipleship.

---

[5] Pope Benedict XVI, God is Love *Deus Caritas Est* (December 25, 2005), § 1, available from http://www.vatican.va.

[6] Pope Benedict XVI, The Sacrament of Charity *Sacramentum Caritatis* (February 22, 2007), § 84, available from http://www.vatican.va.

[7] Allen H. Vigneron, *Unleash the Gospel* (June 3, 2017), 4.2, http://www.unleashthegospel.org.

Decision to Follow Jesus with Determination. The second stage of discipleship is a clear decision to follow Jesus, and to do so with determination. The counter-example of the rich young man in the Gospel demonstrates this. This wealthy young man assures Jesus that he has kept the commandments all his life. He then asks Jesus what he still lacks. "Jesus said to him, 'If you desire to be perfect, go, sell your possessions and give to the poor, and you will have treasure in heaven; and come, follow me.' Upon hearing this word, the young man went away sad, for he had great possessions" (Matt 19:21–22).

Jesus placed a high bar before this young would-be disciple. The man needed not just to live a good life, but to set out and follow Jesus with determination and at great personal cost. He counted the cost and found himself unable or unwilling to make the sacrifice. At least he had the honesty to recognize that he could not (at that time) become a disciple of Jesus. He was not willing to pay the cost. Jesus himself draws our attention to counting the cost of following him:

> For which of you, intending to build a tower, does not first sit down and estimate the cost, to see whether he has enough to complete it? Otherwise, when he has laid a foundation and is not able to finish, all who see it will begin to ridicule him, saying, "This fellow began to build and was not able to finish." (Luke 14:28–30, NRSVCE)

Today we are calling this decision to follow Jesus with determination "intentional discipleship." In the Evangelical

Protestant world, Dallas Willard raised this banner, calling Christians to recover the path of intentional discipleship by embracing what he calls "apprenticeship to Jesus":

> But in the last analysis we fail to be disciples only because we do not decide to be. We do not intend to be disciples. It is the power of the decision and the intention over our life that is missing. We should apprentice ourselves to Jesus in a solemn moment, and we should let those around us know that we have done so.[8]

In a Catholic context, Sherry Weddell has likewise demonstrated the importance of recovering "intentional discipleship" in the Church today. She defines intentional discipleship as "a conscious commitment to follow Jesus in the midst of his Church as an obedient disciple and to reorder one's life accordingly."[9]

There is no escaping this threshold of decision. Jesus did not spare those who approached him then and neither does he spare us today. Certainly he waits for the right time and provides the grace. But he also calls and asks us to count (and pay) the cost. This decision to follow Christ is not something to be dreaded or avoided. We have been given the tremendous privilege of choosing to follow Christ. Nothing we will ever do can be more

---

[8] Dallas Willard, *The Divine Conspiracy: Rediscovering Our Hidden Life In God* (New York: HarperCollins, 1998), 298.

[9] Sherry A. Weddell, *Forming Intentional Disciples: The Path to Knowing and Following Jesus* (Huntington, IN: Our Sunday Visitor, 2012), 130.

significant than saying yes to Jesus's invitation to follow him as a disciple.

And really—let's be frank—we don't have a lot to give to God in return. What do we have that he needs or requires? The one thing we possess, that God himself puts into our hands, is our own lives. This we can withhold—we can hang onto our lives and seek our own happiness on our own terms. But we also can, by the grace of God, give our lives away, hand them over to Christ our Master, and become his apprentices. It is by counting the cost, abandoning our lives, and setting out with Jesus that true joy can be ours. As Dallas Willard rightly says, "Counting the cost is precisely what the man with the pearl and the hidden treasure did. Out of it came their decisiveness and joy. It is decisiveness and joy that are the outcomes of the counting."[10]

Facing a Crossroads and Continuing. There is a third stage in the life of costly discipleship that all will face in one way or another. At some point, having set out on the road of discipleship with determination, we will face a crossroads. We will be tempted to turn back, to find another way, to wonder whether this really is the right path. Facing and conquering this temptation is a crucial step and is part of the cost of discipleship. Even in Jesus's own life we can see this crossroads. At the start of his ministry, right after his baptism, Jesus is led into the desert to be tempted by the devil. He is faced with three discrete temptations and he refuses them all. From there he sets out with determination to follow the path that the Father has set for

---

[10] Willard, *The Divine Conspiracy*, 293.

him—and he walks this path down to the final week of his earthly life. But then, right near the end as the climax of his life's work approaches, he is faced with the temptation (again) to seek another way, to dodge the costly path of discipleship laid out before him. Jesus said: "Abba, Father, all things are possible for you; take this cup away from me; yet not what I will, but what you will" (Mark 14:36). This was a severe temptation, yet Jesus faced it and continued on the path of faithful obedience that won the salvation of the world.

We see the same pattern in the lives of Jesus's disciples. In John chapter six, Jesus speaks in provocative language about the need to eat his flesh and drink his blood. Not surprisingly, some of his disciples had a hard time with this language: "Hearing this, many of his disciples said, 'This is a hard word. Who can accept it?'" (John 6:60). As a result, they drew back and no longer followed him as disciples. They reached a crossroads and decided not to continue. At this point we might have expected Jesus to plead with his other disciples to remain with him, but instead he puts the question right in their faces, asking whether they too want to leave him. Peter, responding for himself and the twelve, does not hesitate: "Lord, to whom shall we go? You have the words of eternal life, and we have believed and come to know that you are the Holy One of God" (John 6:68). They pass the test. They decide to continue even though they don't understand the full meaning of Jesus's words and don't really grasp what is in store for Jesus or themselves.

Let's view this "discipleship crossroads" through the lens of the fictional character Sam Gamgee in *The Lord of the Rings.* Sam made a conscious and determined decision to set out with Frodo right from the start, knowing very little about what lay ahead but resolved to stay by the side of his master. Time and again he remained with him throughout the quest. Then, just as the climax of the story approaches, Sam is faced with a crossroads. In a remarkable piece of psychological drama, J. R. R. Tolkien allows us to listen in on Sam's inner dialogue as he fights with despair.

> "So that was the job I felt I had to do when I started," thought Sam: "to help Mr. Frodo to the last step and then die with him? Well, if that is the job then I must do it. But I would dearly like to see Bywater again, and Rosie Cotton and her brothers, and the Gaffer and Marigold and all."
> . . . But even as hope died in Sam, or seemed to die, it was turned to a new strength. Sam's plain hobbit-face grew stern, almost grim, as the will hardened in him, and he felt through all his limbs a thrill, as if he was turning into some creature of stone and steel that neither despair nor weariness nor endless barren miles could subdue.[11]

From this point onwards, the temptation to turn back or give up no longer has any purchase on Sam. He has passed the test and will carry on until he either completes the quest or dies trying.

---

[11] J. R. R. Tolkien, *The Return of the King* (New York: Ballantine Books, 1965), 234.

THE KEY TO DISCIPLESHIP:
OFFERING OUR LIVES

Each of us can ask, "Where am I on the path of discipleship?" and "What is the next step for me to take?" Perhaps you are like one of the people in the crowds that gathered to see and hear Jesus. You are "nearby," checking things out and interested, but you have not personally encountered Jesus. The next step is to seek to know the Lord Jesus personally and to take the steps that will encourage this encounter.[12] Or maybe you have experienced the presence of Jesus and the work of the Spirit in your life, but you haven't found a way to follow-up on this. Either you have never been shown the path of discipleship or you have some obstacle that is preventing you from stepping onto that path with determination. Or perhaps you have been following the path of discipleship for some time but have encountered some trial or grief that has put you at a crossroads. Like Peter and the twelve, your next step is to seek and act upon the grace to continue and so enter into the deeper path of discipleship that lies ahead.

Whatever stage we may be in, the critical response for us to make *at every stage* is an offering of our lives to the Lord. We could also call this *a full consecration of our lives to the Lord*. We don't need to be perfect to do this (not one of us is). We don't need to have our lives in excellent order or have complete emotional stability. With the help of God—by his grace—we can take our lives as they are and hand them fully over to the Lord for his disposal. This

---

[12] There are many vehicles that can help this personal encounter, including the Life in the Spirit Seminars and the Alpha Course.

is the *response* at every stage that enables us genuinely to be his disciples. The story of the sinful woman anointing Jesus's feet illustrates this act of complete abandonment:

> And a woman in the city, who was a sinner, having learned that he was eating in the Pharisee's house, brought an alabaster jar of ointment. She stood behind him at his feet, weeping, and began to bathe his feet with her tears and to dry them with her hair. Then she continued kissing his feet and anointing them with the ointment. (Luke 7:37–38, NRSVCE)

This woman was not living a holy life—Jesus says a few verses later that her sins were many (Luke 7:47). But in full-hearted repentance she pours out the precious oil upon the Lord, a sign of her full consecration and her offering of love. Jesus gladly receives this offering, forgives her sins, and praises her action.

Many obstacles can stand in the way of making this full and "costly" offering of our lives to Christ. For some of us, we lack the *maturity* to take hold of our lives and offer them to the Lord. We can't give away what we don't have. Some of us are bound up with various *fears and anxieties*. We are worried about our lives, what living for God might demand of us, and so we hold back. We may need prayer for deliverance from these binding fears, but we also need that adventurous faith that steps out and makes the full offering of our lives.

Some of us are captive to habits and addictions that bind us with cords; they oppress us, condemn us, and so keep us from giving our lives to Christ fully. As it says in 2 Peter, "whatever it is that overcomes someone, to that he is enslaved" (2 Pet 2:19). Whether it be to alcohol, drugs, pornography, or something else, these ingrained habits can prevent us from offering our lives fully to the Lord God. The good news is that Jesus came to deliver us all from the power of sinful habits; he has the power to break through these and help us gain steady victory over them. The good news is that Christ Jesus has "overcome the world" and all its powers (John 16:33). If we are willing to pay the cost, we can gain greater freedom, step-by-step, from habits and addictions.

The road to full and complete freedom in Christ will occupy all our lives and we will only reach this goal in eternal life. But the path begins now. By his help and grace, we can count the cost and respond to his call with adventurous faith. What the Lord has in store for you, only he knows. What a marvelous adventure lies ahead in finding out! But Jesus only asks for what we can—by his grace—offer to him. He doesn't ask the impossible from us, but gives us steps that we can actually take. Let's take the step the Lord presents to us: to set out on the path of discipleship; to continue on it with zeal; to take the hard road at the crossroads and stay on the path. And most of all, let's count the cost and decide to pay it. Let's offer our lives as fully and completely to the Lord as we can, using the freedom he has given us to hand ourselves over to him, and to know the deep joy of the Lord in this offering of our lives.

* *Portrait* *

FR. DAMIEN OF MOLOKAI

I can recall when I came across the life of Fr. Damien of Molokai for the first time. I was in my early twenties, and I became fascinated with this Belgian priest who gave up everything, not only to serve God's people, but to throw himself into a challenging mission in Hawaii far away from home. All this was most impressive in itself. But then came the day when the civil authorities decided that missionaries could no longer come and go among the lepers on the island of Molokai. The danger was too great; the chance of catching and spreading the dread disease was too high. And so the leader of Damien's mission, a veteran priest and missionary, announced to the gathered missionaries that, if the leper colony was to have access to a priest, one of them would have to go there *and never return*. Never.

He told the missionaries that he would not demand this sacrifice from any of them; it must be a freewill offering. *Three* priest-missionaries volunteered straight away, Damien and two others. But Damien argued his case based on his broad experience and strong physical stature, and he was elected to go. I recall my eyes filling with tears as I read this account. Here is a man who—in one instant—gives his entire life away. But of course it was not just the decision of the moment: Fr. Damien had been preparing for this all his adult life by the choices he made to give all to Christ and hold nothing back. When the hour came he was ready.

Fr. Damien labored among the lepers for many years, finally catching the deadly disease and succumbing to its ravages. He counted the cost and gladly paid the price, dying out of love for his Lord and all the lepers that he served. The crown is now his.

·✻·

CHAPTER FOUR

RoboCop, Superheroes, and
the Incarnation

The eternal Word became small—small enough to
fit into a manger. He became a child, so that the
word could be grasped by us. Now the word is not
simply audible; not only does it have a *voice*, now
the word has a *face*, one which we can see: that of
Jesus of Nazareth.

—Pope Benedict XVI[1]

THIS chapter seeks to answer two basic questions: (1)
Who is Jesus Christ? and (2) What did he come to do?
In other words, it covers the doctrines of the Incarnation
and the Redemption, core beliefs for the Christian faith.
But we are going to arrive at answers to these questions
through unusual means. By looking at contemporary,
"secular" versions of what a human being should be, and

---

[1] Pope Benedict XVI, The Word of the Lord *Verbum Domini* (September 30, 2010), § 12, available from http://www.vatican.va.

THE ADVENTURE OF DISCIPLESHIP

especially by investigating our cultural fascination with superheroes, we will try to discern how these portrayals of human destiny both point to and fall short of a Christian understanding. In other words, by comparison and contrast with contemporary representations of human fulfillment in modern media, I hope to illuminate a fresh path to the core doctrines of our faith.

At the same time, we will be returning to the astounding claim, noted in the first chapter, that the author of the story of our world *entered* that story and became its main character. The author stepped into his own narrative and really became its primary "player." Did he do this like a superhero coming to the rescue of the people? Or did he come in some other, more wonderful way—a way that reveals our true destiny?

This examination of who Jesus is and what he has done for us is not a departure from our topic (the costly adventure of discipleship). How can we follow someone and offer our lives to him without reserve if we don't know who he is? How can we cooperate with his work in us and carry out that work in the world if we don't know what he came to do? Someone might reasonably ask: *Then why didn't you begin with this? Wouldn't it make sense to start with who Jesus is and what he has done before talking about what it means to follow him on the road of costly discipleship?* Yes, normally we would begin with these questions. But for two reasons I have delayed treating these questions until now.

First, the entry-point for this book is the love of adventure—with Christianity as the great and true adventure—and it was important to establish this first and describe what it means. The goal was to gain a new angle on our faith and what it means to embrace the call to discipleship. But second, many people are drawn to Christianity and initially commit themselves to it *before* they have a deep and full understanding of who Jesus is and what he has done for us. In fact, *all* the first disciples fall into this category. They clearly did not know who Jesus was when they began to follow him—this was only gradually revealed to them—and they didn't realize the truth fully until he rose from the dead. At the start, they certainly did not know what he had come to do and how he was going to do it. Peter even tried to prevent him from going to the Cross.

We assume that most people come to faith in Christ through an orderly process of sorting through all the questions, examining all the doctrines, and then deciding that they believe it is all true. Well, some people do approach the question of belief in this way, but they are the minority (and besides, faith is always a gift, never simply an intellectual conclusion). Most people are drawn to believe by contact with other Christians or by an answered prayer or by the magnetism of the person of Christ, and only *after* they come to believe initially do they actively seek to *understand* their faith more fully. Rodney Stark, a sociologist of religion, claims that studies of conversion in contemporary religious movements show that most people pursue doctrinal understanding only after they experience some kind of conversion: "Modern social science relegates doctrinal appeal to a very secondary role, claiming that most people do not really become very attached to the doctrines of their new faith until *after* their conversion."[2] Doctrine is important—in fact, essential—but most people delve into doctrinal matters only after they have set out, initially at least, on the path of discipleship.

ROBOCOP AND SUPERHEROES

Years ago when living in England I found myself sitting on a London Underground platform, waiting for my train to arrive. Like all travelers, my eyes turned to the advertisements that surrounded me. Right in front of me was a large poster advertising the movie *RoboCop*. The catchphrase caught my attention: "Part man, part machine, all cop." I thought about this and pondered—and pondered some more. My mind began to race across a vast set of contemporary figures and images. All the superheroes I had loved as a boy appeared before my mind: Superman, Batman, Green Lantern, Spiderman, the Fantastic Four, the X-Men, and others. I asked myself these questions: What do all these strange and wonderful creations of our minds reveal about our hopes and dreams? Why do we find them so endlessly fascinating? I began to notice something: the superheroes that we dream up always have something "greater" about them, but at the same time they remain human. We want them to have special powers and abilities that enable them to do great (and cool) things, but equally we desperately need them to remain human at the same time. We don't tend to create non-human superheroes (though they exist). When we create non-human

---

[2] Rodney Stark, *The Rise of Christianity* (San Francisco: HarperCollins, 1997), 14–15.

superheroes or science-fiction characters, they tend to be, paradoxically, "human" in some way.

Why are we fascinated with the superhero? Why do we keep on creating characters who are human and yet at the same time superhuman? I believe it is because there is something good and right about our humanness but also something lacking. We long to be what we are (that is, human) but we also long to be much more than we are (that is, to be superhuman). The heroes we create reflect this longing to be something more, something greater, yet at the same time to remain the human beings that we are.

Back to RoboCop. He was described as "part man, part machine, all cop." We don't want a simple robot to do our policing. We want someone human who is more than human—someone who is part machine. I think back to the fascination we had in my youth with the "Six Million Dollar Man" and the "Bionic Woman." We want humanity, but we desire much more than just our lowly humanity. We want a humanity that is more powerful, more capable, able to overcome our present limitations. Our superheroes express a deep longing for our own fulfillment—but of course they do so only partially and imperfectly. They don't and can't reveal the full vision of what we are meant to be.

THE SUPERHERO PARADIGM

Superheroes come in all sizes and shapes. Through the multiplication of superhero movies, they have become a kind of primary lens through which we look at ourselves: our hopes, our issues, our problems, our failures, our longings. Every sort of social and moral issue can be represented and examined in the superhero drama, even if they normally portray these superficially. They display for us the "adventure" that we all seek and enable us to taste the adventure that eludes us in our ordinary lives.

Occasionally, the superhero story is really just about the battle between a given superhero and his nemesis—a kind of personal battle between two powerful foes, with the populace looking on. But far more often, the superhero story expresses this common paradigm: an evil villain arises who endangers the wider populace (and usually the whole human race), and normal law enforcement has no chance against the superpowers of the villain. And so the superhero appears on the scene, often reluctantly, to do battle with the villain and overcome him (or her). The bulk of the story is all about how the superhero overcomes the enemy against all odds. And when the superhero has triumphed, however tragically, equilibrium and peace is restored to the world—and the superhero goes off into seclusion or attempts to carry on "normal life" until a new foe arises. This is the basic plot line—and it works. We are hooked by the hopelessness of the problem, foolishly worried whether the superhero will really be able to overcome evil this time, and greatly relieved when the deed is done. We seem to never tire of having this plot told and retold in endless variety.

The crucial thing to notice is that the end-game of the superhero paradigm is basic peace and order. The goal of the superhero plot is to return things to their normal and orderly state. Okay—sometimes we witness general improvement of values and opinions as a result of the struggle. But the typical goal is "restoration" of the previous order of ordinary people. Once the task of defeating the evil villain is accomplished, the superhero retires and things go on as they were. We could say that the "end" or *telos* of the superhero narrative is the peace of human society functioning freely and without oppression. Not a bad goal! But far from a Christian view of redemption of the world.

Let's consider two individual examples of this paradigm. In the acclaimed movie, *Batman Begins* (2005), the audience is introduced to Bruce Wayne both as a boy and as a young man who is striving to overcome the fear and guilt that weigh upon him due to the murder of his parents. He is a troubled boy—and a troubled young man—trying to find himself and overcome his fear. The human drama surrounding young Bruce Wayne is impressive. We as the audience are deeply sympathetic with his plight, cheering for him to fight through and face his fears.

The backdrop for the narrative is the city of Gotham, falling ever deeper into corruption, crime, and destitution. Through the efforts of Bruce Wayne's parents, Gotham had been doing well. But now that they are off the scene, the city has crumbled and is pitching headlong into unrecoverable corruption. Gotham City and its people are the *problem* that needs a solution. Who will save the city? Rachel Dawes, Bruce's boyhood companion, is an earnest, energetic district attorney, fighting (helplessly) against the wall of corruption. She also serves as Bruce's conscience, calling him to leave behind his fear and anger and act on behalf of the city. But it is obvious that Rachel cannot save Gotham City on her own.

Bruce Wayne then goes underground, seeking some kind of salvation by mixing and mingling among the criminal classes. Eventually, he ends up in an unnamed

Asian country where he is approached and recruited by Ra's al Ghul, who trains him in the highest form of the martial arts. This is one part of the "superpowers" that Wayne attains. He becomes a great fighter, a living weapon, who can overcome nearly any human foe. For his part, Ra's al Ghul also has a plan for Gotham City: he believes that it must be utterly destroyed and built new from the ground—and he hopes to win Bruce Wayne to his cause. Wayne refuses—he leaves amidst a bloody battle and returns to Gotham City to undertake his own way of "saving" the city from corruption. There he runs across a specialist in his company who introduces him to the most developed military weapons and gadgets ever produced. This is the other half of Batman's superpowers: he has an arsenal, a motorized vehicle (the Batmobile), and high-tech equipment that enable him to do far more than a normal human being could accomplish.

What then unfolds is a complex plot in which Ra's al Ghul returns (with his cronies) to bring about the destruction of the city, even as Wayne (now Batman) is fighting to rid the city of its entrenched criminals and corrupt officials. The inevitable showdown between Batman and his former trainer provides the climax of the film. And unsurprisingly, Batman wins the contest and saves the city from destruction. But things are never that simple when sequels must be produced. So we find that a hoard of criminally insane characters was released from a mental hospital, setting the stage for the arrival of the Joker and the plot for the next film.

Batman Begins is a highly effective example of the superhero paradigm. The city of Gotham is threatened, millions of lives are at stake, and a solution must be found. Two opposing answers clash—and the audience is meant to identify with the solution proposed by Batman, however imperfect and slow in execution. Through a series of encounters in which Batman must use all his prowess, his gadgets, and his wits and courage, our superhero defeats the powerful villain and (for a short time) the city is saved. The people can go on with their normal lives, free of the threat of imminent destruction.

The film *Captain America and the Winter Soldier* (2014) provides another twist on the superhero paradigm. Captain America was the original Marvel Comics superhero, first appearing during the Second World War (1941) as a kind of super-soldier in the fight against Nazism. The protagonist, Steve Rogers, experiences the kind of mythic transformation that we all long for. In himself, he is weak, unexceptional, unable to keep up with the other soldiers. But thanks to a new and secret serum injected into his body, he becomes the muscled athlete, able to run faster and jump higher than any normal human being, and wielding a powerful shield that he skillfully employs as a defensive and offensive weapon. Every scrawny boy dreams of imitating this complete transformation from weakling to super-athlete and fighter.

Frozen in suspended animation for decades, Steve Rogers thaws out and reappears in the early twenty-first century, now facing the battles of our age. And Captain America is reborn. The plot of *Captain America and the Winter Soldier* has a special twist, a favorite of modern audiences. The great evil villain is not just a foe "out there"—we quickly learn that the "good guys" (S.H.I.E.L.D.) have been infiltrated by the terrorist network, Hydra, and in fact have been the puppet of Hydra from the beginning. It dawns on our heroes that all their efforts to do good have really been at the service of their enemy—they have been hoodwinked and outflanked at every turn.

The *problem* to be solved is the launching of three coordinated super-ships that will circle the earth, directed by satellites, and kill whomever the "bad guys" desire. Through the use of these super-ships, Hydra plans to run the world and control every aspect of human life. This is the classic superhero paradigm: the bad guys are soon to be in charge with tools to control the whole world and no one is able to stop them. That is, until Steve Rogers as Captain America decides to resist. Warned by the dying words of his boss (who in the end did not die), Rogers goes rogue, and with the help of two companions, sets out to foil the unstoppable plans of Hydra. From here the plot unfolds replete with clever twists and heart-racing battle scenes. In the end, unsurprisingly, Hydra is defeated, the traitors of Hydra are killed, and Captain America and his allies win the day.

It is the kind of story we love to see: the superhero, who is basically a good and upright man, opposes powerful, overwhelming forces, and the world is once again saved from destruction, so that normal people can go about their lives free of oppression and danger. But of course there is a hook that sets up the sequel: Captain America has defeated his nemesis—the Winter Soldier—for the time being, but in the final scene he sets out to find this soldier—who incidentally is *part man and part machine*—to "redeem" him from the brainwashing he has endured at the hands of Hydra. The human side of Captain America, expressed in his loyalty and friendship for his closest friend in World War II, brings the film to a satisfying close.

The enormous popularity of superhero comics and movies demonstrates that we are drawn to them like magnets. Our culture gladly embraces endless refractions of this basic story. And crucial to the attraction of the superhero is the combination of superpowers with real human qualities. We can identify with these superheroes because they are human like we are: they make mistakes, they have fears, and they wrestle with personal problems and relationship issues. Despite their superpowers they are vulnerable—as we are—in one way or another. Even Superman, possessing perhaps the greatest of all powers, falls sick and in danger of death in the presence of kryptonite. At the same time, we are drawn to and mesmerized by their powers and abilities, physical and intellectual. They seem to draw us upwards and lift us into a world that, all too briefly, transcends our normal, mundane lives.

JESUS IS NOT A SUPERHERO

As it turns out, many people basically adopt something like this superhero view of Jesus and what he came to do. Surveying the religious beliefs of teenagers, Christian Smith summarized their basic theistic worldview as "moral therapeutic deism."[3] What he means by this is that most

---

[3] See Christian Smith and Melina Lundquist Denton, *Soul Searching: The Religious Lives of American Teenagers* (Oxford: Oxford University Press, 2005).

young people believe God wants us to be good ("moral"), and that God is mainly there to help me with my personal needs ("therapeutic"), but that otherwise God just leaves us to get on with our lives ("deism"). Most people believe in God—he is good and watches over things. But he doesn't need to be particularly involved in our life unless things go really wrong. When we have a problem, that's when we call upon God and he comes to help—and then he goes off again to a safe and convenient distance, leaving us to go on with life on our own terms. This is really a superhero view of God.

Is the superhero paradigm a good model for the redemption that Jesus came to bring? Is he just the greatest of the superheroes? Not really. While there are some similarities, Jesus is not a superhero. From the perspective of Christian faith, the human race has a massive problem that needs solving. The Apostle Paul sums up the main elements of our problem very concisely:

> You were dead through the trespasses and sins in which you once lived, following the course of this world, following the ruler of the power of the air, the spirit that is now at work among those who are disobedient. All of us once lived among them in the passions of our flesh, following the desires of flesh and senses, and we were by nature children of wrath, like everyone else. (Eph 2:1–3, NRSVCE)

This is our predicament: we are slaves of sin and can't escape by our own efforts. We stand under the sentence of death and can't evade it. We live under the dominion of the devil, unable to overcome him by our own powers. It is from these that Jesus came to deliver us.

But notice: he didn't just swoop down from the sky, defeat our enemies in a furious battle, and then retreat back to his own place. In order to redeem us, the eternal Son of God actually *became one of us*—not as a disguise or as a temporary identity, but so that he could renovate our nature from within. He didn't just come to defeat our enemies and leave us in peace; he came to change us inside and out, to bring about a new creation. And he himself—Jesus, the Son of God—is the beginning of that new creation.

In the superhero paradigm, once the enemy has been defeated, we go back to our normal lives, free from oppression (for the time being). That's far better than living under the oppression of a tyrant. But Christ came to bring us so much more. Salvation in Christ means being joined to him and becoming part of his body. He doesn't just restore things to a peaceable order; he brings about a new creation. Jesus didn't come on a special ops mission—a sting operation—and then withdraw to leave us in peace. *He is our peace!* We have life by being joined to him, and through the Spirit we are made into his image and likeness.

Have you ever heard the slogan that says, "Christians aren't perfect, just forgiven"? Well, we certainly aren't perfect—not yet. But we are far more than just forgiven. If we are "just forgiven," just reinstated to where we were before, then we remain unchanged and all our enemies can still gain power over us again. God our Father has much more in store for us, his sons and daughters, than just forgiveness.

We profoundly need to be forgiven, but we are also called and empowered to be transformed (Rom 8:29), to become new beings (2 Cor 5:17), to be perfect and complete like our heavenly Father is perfect (Matt 5:48). None of this happens in the superhero version of Christian faith. For this to happen we need a living Christ, active in our lives. We need to have our lives be "in Christ," his life becoming ours: "I am the vine, you are the branches. The one who abides in me, and I in him, bears much fruit, for apart from me you can do nothing" (John 15:5).

It is a curious fact that superheroes don't need to love the people they protect and save. They don't even need to like them very much, and they certainly don't have to live among them. Commonly, superheroes "enter the fray" and confront evil somewhat reluctantly. They do so because they see a desperate need or because they feel an obligation to help because of their superpowers. Only rarely do they show genuine love for the people they are serving, and when this happens it is often because they become romantically entangled with non-superheroes. The contrast with our heavenly Father and the Son he sent couldn't be sharper: "For God so loved the world, that he gave his only Son, that whoever believes in him should not perish but have eternal life" (John 3:16, ESV). Paul reminds us that Christ loved us even when we were his enemies, when we rejected him entirely: "Why, one will hardly die for a righteous man—though perhaps for a good man one will dare even to die. But God shows his love for us in that while we were yet sinners Christ died for us" (Rom 5:7–8, RSVCE). God sent his Son out of love for us, even when we did not merit this love. And after saving us, he does not withdraw and leave us to ourselves, but draws us to himself. The good news of the Gospel is that God himself is the source of our life: "I came that they may have life, and have it abundantly" (John 10:10, ESV). God himself has given us eternal life through the gift of his Son (1 John 5:11).

THE GLORIOUS TRUTH OF
THE INCARNATION

Back to the London Underground platform. It struck me quite suddenly, on that day waiting for the train, that hidden within the images of RoboCop and other superheroes was a longing for something that was truly realized only in *the Incarnation of the Son of God*. Our invention of superheroes expresses a deep yearning to find fulfillment in something greater, and yet to remain what we are—that is, human beings. Isn't this just what the Christian doctrine of the Incarnation reveals in a consummate way? When I think of the Incarnation—the descent of the eternal Son of God into our world, into time and history—I am struck by the parallel with the human author of a story deciding to enter that story himself and become one of its own characters. But the author of this story—the living God—created a *real* world by his word that has real characters with real minds and real wills. And it was into this world that this author decided to "descend" and take up a genuine role in human history, within the limits of time and space.

The Son of God took on the poverty of our human condition in order to raise us to the riches of his divine life (2 Cor 8:9). And yet he didn't just *appear* in human form as a kind of disguise to do a job. The humanity of

Jesus is not just a set of clothes that he put on and then took off. He isn't like the aliens in the movie *Men in Black* who possess human bodies. Our faith tells us that Christ really became a man—a genuine human being—in order to renovate and renew our humanity from within.

RoboCop is "part man, part machine." But Christ is not "part man, part God." He is fully man, fully God, and entirely our Redeemer. In fact, Christians in the early Church flirted with this composite model of the Incarnation, that the Jesus of the Gospels is part man and part God. But this was rightly seen as inadequate. He is not a midway point between man and God, half of each but not fully either one. No, he remains fully God while becoming fully a human being—he joins the two by being fully both.

To say this differently: Jesus was sent by the Father to show us who we truly are. He didn't just win a victory; he revealed what it is to be a human being. He didn't just provide us with a model to follow (though he certainly did do that); he came to make us new. We can imitate him and follow his model only by being joined to him and by freely cooperating with his grace and power in our own transformation. And crucially, when he rose from the dead he didn't leave our nature behind, but died and rose again *in our nature*. Jesus did not "wear" our human nature for a season and then cast it off. Even now, we believe, he lives in a glorified human nature—and this is what we are called to share in.

Superheroes, and, in fact, many science-fiction characters, contain within them elements of truth and reflect in a partial way the longing in our hearts to be something more—to find fulfillment in something beyond what we now experience. But even as they point to what we long for, they fall short of that goal. Only in the person of Jesus do we find the true fulfillment of our longings. Only in the Incarnation of the Son of God and the new life he brings can we achieve the transformation that God, the author of the story, has in store for us. Jesus doesn't just return us to a state of peace and normality and leave us as we were; he triumphs over sin and death in us, makes us each into a "new creation" (2 Cor 5:17), and brings into being a new community called the Church that will live with him and in him for all eternity. This is what God has in store for us in his Son.

* *Portrait* *
MOTHER TERESA OF CALCUTTA

Mother Teresa hardly fits the portrait of a superhero. She had no special physical or psychic abilities or powers. She did not confront evil and overthrow it by a show of force. In fact, she was a short, slight, and unimposing person. And yet she displays in a marvelous way what the follower of Christ is to be. She came to know that real transformation and power is achieved by allowing Christ to dwell fully in her and to offer herself completely for Christ. In her case, this meant giving herself in a radical way to the poorest of the poor. Through her own example and through the religious order she founded, Mother Teresa became a source of inspiration to many. But if we look more deeply, we see something much more than someone doing good things for others. We now know that she suffered deeply in the life she chose to live—she knew the reality of the cross profoundly. In the deeply etched lines of her face, we can see the costly beauty of a life ventured for Christ. Through the offering of her life, she herself was transformed to be like Christ, and she served this transformation in the lives of so many others, especially of the poor. Mother Teresa models for us what it means to allow the "supernatural" power of Christ to invade our lives and make them new.

·❧·

CHAPTER FIVE

Providence, Hope, and the Gift of the Spirit

Divine providence works also through the actions of creatures. To human beings God grants the ability to cooperate freely with his plans.

—CCC 323

The uncertainty of human existence cannot be totally removed. But it can be "overcome"—by hope and only by hope.

—Josef Pieper[1]

We live in an anxious world. Concern and worry about the most basic things surrounds us all. But when has this not been true? Ever since Adam and Eve departed from the Garden, anxiety has been our constant companion. How will we survive? What will we eat? Whom will we marry? And so on.

---

[1] Josef Pieper, *Faith, Hope, Love* (San Francisco: Ignatius Press, 1997), 129.

Jesus recognized and spoke directly to this basic anxiety in his teaching in the Sermon on the Mount. "Therefore I tell you, do not be anxious about your life, what you shall eat or what you shall drink, nor about your body, what you shall put on" (Matt 6:25). On the one hand, being anxious doesn't do us any good. Which of us, by giving way to anxiety, can add anything to our span of life? (Matt 6:27). But more importantly, Jesus assures us that we have a heavenly Father—a provident Father—who watches out for us and will take care of us: "Therefore do not worry, saying, 'What will we eat?' or 'What will we drink?' or 'What will we wear?' For it is the Gentiles who strive for all these things; and indeed your heavenly Father knows that you need all these things" (Matt 6:31–32, NRSVCE).

The Apostle Paul, too, urges us to put away our anxieties by placing our needs and requests before the living God: "Do not be anxious about anything, but in everything by prayer and supplication with thanksgiving let your requests be made known to God" (Phil 4:6, ESV). What is the result if we do this? The peace of God, which surpasses all our understanding or expectation, will guard and protect our hearts and minds (Phil 4:7).

We all face the insecurities of human life; we all have to deal with anxieties about what we need for today and tomorrow. But an even deeper and more basic concern gnaws at our hearts. Will my life turn out well? Is there any meaning or significance to my life? Does it really matter whether I live or die? Is there such a thing as right and wrong, and does it matter how I act? Is there any real justice in the world, or are we all part of a meaningless plot that is going nowhere? These are questions that concern hope and despair. Is there anything to hope for, really? Does my life—and the world itself—have any meaning? None of us can thrive for very long without hope, without a sense of meaning.

Have you ever, while watching a movie, found yourself wondering if the plot is going to be resolved? A few years back I was watching a contemporary "western" with friends. As the plot progressed, a burning question loomed over the story and all its anxiety-ridden characters: would they find their way through the dangerous land they were crossing to the safe land beyond, or would they all die from lack of water or through ambush from enemies? As the plot slowly (and painfully) developed, I began to suspect that this was one of those movies in which the screenwriter, director, and producer were intentionally conspiring together to frustrate the normal expectations of the viewers. It dawned on me that there wasn't going to be any resolution to the plot. Sure enough, the movie came to a sudden end with no resolution and no expectation of ever finding out what happened. We were left—along with the characters in the story—in suspense. There wasn't even a hint of resolution. We all spontaneously hooted and hollered at the screen; one young man (fittingly, in my view) threw his shoe toward the screen in disgust.

One mark of great adventures is the presence of a "providence" surrounding the story and its characters. Most often this providential hand remains hidden, operating behind the scenes. Nonetheless, the characters are often able to perceive this hand of providence at work at least at key points, and the readers (or viewers) of the story recognize that there is some purpose, some guiding hand, that drives the story. There is, at the very least, a sense of meaning or purpose in the story. Why are all true adventures governed by this sense of providence or of purpose? Because they are reflecting *the* great adventure—the story of the Gospel—which is governed by the providence of God our Father.

In a great adventure, despite real losses and setbacks, the virtue of *hope* is in play. This is a hope that, despite all appearances, something good will come. There is a reason for struggling and fighting; there is hope that justice will eventually prevail. If not, why bother fighting and struggling at all? In fact, as audiences gather to watch blockbuster movies, they *bring with them* the expectation that there is a point and purpose to the drama that will unfold, something good that will come from all the fighting and loss and bloodshed and sorrow.

The aim of this chapter is to illustrate, through comparison and contrast, the activity of providence and the presence of hope in selected adventures and authors, and then to show how the story of the Gospel exemplifies the qualities of providence and hope to the highest degree. Our consideration of providence will eventually lead us to take up the central (and essential) revelation of God as our Father and to recognize the role of the Holy Spirit as our advocate, counselor, and guide. By viewing these subjects through the lens of "adventure," the goal is to deepen our grasp of familiar Christian truths and to help us embrace, *with grounded hope*, the challenging and perplexing aspects of the costly adventure of discipleship.

PROVIDENCE IN *THE HORSE AND HIS BOY*

One of the most beloved of C. S. Lewis's Chronicles of Narnia is the story of Shasta and Bree in *The Horse and His Boy*. From the opening line we are left in no doubt that an "adventure" lies before us: "This is the story of an adventure that happened in Narnia and Calormen and the lands between, in the Golden Age when Peter was High King in Narnia and his brother and his two sisters were King and Queens under him."[2] We are immediately introduced to Shasta, a young boy living a grim and tedious life with a father who beats him at regular intervals. But Shasta has one source of hope in his life: he longs to discover what lies to the north of his home. He is drawn to an unnamed and unknown "hope" that pulls at his heart. In just a few pages, the adventure is framed and underway: Shasta is to be sold to a nobleman who appears on the scene; he learns that the nobleman's horse actually can talk; and the horse and boy agree to escape together and set out secretly to find the promised land of Narnia in the north.

Lewis tells a marvelous tale that includes delightful characters, mistaken identities, captures and escapes, and a climax in which Shasta plays the hero's role. It's a rags-to-riches story of the best kind: the untutored boy turns out to be the crown prince, who, in fact, acts more courageously than those better trained and equipped. But it is also the story of the unfolding of a providential hand that guides the action from beginning to end. Lewis decided to display "providence" in this story with particular clarity, especially to the reader, though the characters in the story

---

[2] C. S. Lewis, *The Horse and His Boy* (New York: HarperCollins, 1982), 1.

eventually realize the providential guide that has been at work throughout.

Providence appears in the form of a "cat" or "lion" that repeatedly shows up and guides the story in decisive ways. Readers familiar with the Narnia books of course recognize early on that this "cat" is really Aslan, the divine figure who drives all the Narnia stories. It first appears as a lion chasing Shasta and Bree. The result of their flight is that they meet up with Aravis and her talking horse, Hwin. The meeting of the two fugitive pairs will prove crucial to the execution of the plot. Next, a large "cat" appears when Shasta is all alone at night among the tombs. It guides him to a safe place, provides a warm back against which he lies down, and (in the form of a lion) chases off threatening hyenas. Then, at the crucial turn in the story, the lion appears again, chasing our characters forward and seeming to attack Aravis. Through this "attack" the lion (Aslan) pushed them forward at the pivotal moment so that the warning would be given in time.

Finally, Shasta finds himself all alone at night on a mountain pass, buried in deep fog. Lo and behold, the lion appears once again walking by his side. Terrified but unable to flee, Shasta in desperation asks, "Who are you?" The Lion responds: "One who has waited long for you to speak." Still fearful, Shasta begs Aslan to go away and leave him alone: "Oh, please—please do go away. What harm have I ever done you? Oh, I am the unluckiest person in the whole world." The Lion invites Shasta to tell his troubles, and so Shasta recounts the woeful story of his life, highlighting the "persecution" he has experienced from lions all throughout the journey. In turn, the Lion answers,

"I do not call you unfortunate." Shasta replies: "Don't you think it was bad luck to meet so many lions?" Aslan replies: "There was only one lion." He then unveils the providential hand that has guided Shasta for his entire life.

> I was the lion. . . . I was the lion who forced you to join with Aravis. I was the cat who comforted you among the houses of the dead. I was the lion who drove the jackals from you while you slept. I was the lion who gave the horses new strength of fear for the last mile so that you should reach King Lune in time. And I was the lion you do not remember who pushed the boat in which you lay, a child near death, so that it came to shore where a man sat, wakeful at midnight, to receive you.[3]

What seemed like a series of misfortunes—even persecutions—turns out to be a pattern of providential blessings that guides Shasta toward his true calling. It was prophesied at his birth that he would save his land and people from the greatest peril they would ever face. And the story of *The Horse and His Boy* is the unfolding of that plot whereby Shasta saves his people and his land.

The genius of the story is that, even when the hand of providence is revealed, it is nonetheless Shasta (and the others) who need to act. If they fail to act, the battle is lost. Shasta actually saves the day through great bravery; he needs to press on in perplexity and hardship. Yes, a clear, providential hand guided and protected him. But

[3] Lewis, *The Horse and His Boy*, 183–85.

he is a true actor in the story, not a puppet manipulated by the hand of God. Aslan's interventions do not inhibit Shasta's freedom; they enable him to act freely and heroically. Only at the end does Shasta realize how the hand of providence has been at work: he simply couldn't have seen this until it was revealed at the end. Yet all along, he acted in *hope*, sometimes even demonstrating a "hope against hope" that kept him going even when there seemed little to hope for. In this finely told tale, C. S. Lewis powerfully portrays the action of divine providence—a personal providence, not an impersonal force—that invites, and cooperates with, human freedom.

J. R. R. TOLKIEN AND GEORGE R. R. MARTIN: COMPARISON AND CONTRAST

A contrast between two epic fantasies might be useful for illustrating the critical role of providence and hope in adventures. In *The Lord of the Rings* (and accompanying stories), J. R. R. Tolkien creates a world of tremendous depth with a palate of delightful characters who work together to accomplish a quest that seeks to deliver the world from a great evil.[4] In *A Game of Thrones* (and succeeding volumes), George Martin fashions a tumultuous, complex world of medieval knights and kingdoms vying with one another for rule.[5] Both fantasy worlds have been

---

[4] Tolkien developed his fictional world over many years, and his writings include *The Hobbit*, *The Lord of the Rings*, *The Silmarillion*, and many volumes of unfinished stories and notes.

[5] The overall name for Martin's epic work is *A Song of Ice and Fire*. The first volume in this work, *A Game of Thrones*, is also the name adopted by the popular TV series.

successfully adapted for the screen: Tolkien's trilogy into three blockbuster and award-winning movies, Martin's *A Game of Thrones* into a wildly popular TV series. There are no doubt numerous and interesting parallels and contrasts between the two epic works, but for our purposes I want to limit the comparison to how providence and hope function respectively in the two fantasy worlds.

The Lord of the Rings. The reader of *The Lord of the Rings* has to pay close attention to spot the references to the hand of providence in the story—but they are there. The first examples appear at the beginning when Gandalf is telling Frodo how the Ring came to him and how a great evil has arisen in the world again. Frodo responds, "I wish it need not have happened in my time." And Gandalf quickly counters: "So do I . . . and so do all who live to see such times. But that is not for them to decide. All we have to decide is what to do with the time that is given us."[6] Notice the passive voice: "the time that is given." Clearly there is a "givenness" in this story; the choice the characters face is what to do with the cards they have been dealt.

Gandalf then uses even stronger language about a design that lies behind Frodo coming to possess the Ring: "There was something else at work, beyond any design of the Ring-maker. I can put it no plainer than by saying that Bilbo was *meant* to find the Ring, and *not* by its maker. In which case you were *meant* to have it. And that may be an encouraging thought."[7] Frodo, however is not

6 Tolkien, *The Fellowship of the Ring*, 76.
7 Tolkien, *The Fellowship of the Ring*, 81.

THE ADVENTURE OF DISCIPLESHIP

encouraged—he is dismayed by the dire straits he is in. But both the reader and Frodo are learning that there is a design to what is happening, a *meaning* to all that is going on. The story is not purposeless, aimless, or meaningless. There is a deep significance and a guiding hand at work. Finally, Frodo in exasperation asks, "I wish I had never seen the Ring! Why did it come to me? Why was I chosen?" Gandalf answers, "Such questions cannot be answered. . . . But you have been chosen, and you must therefore use such strength and heart and wits as you have."[8] This is quite striking language: Frodo somehow recognizes that he has been "chosen" by a providential hand. Gandalf agrees but recognizes that they cannot find out how or why—they simply have to press ahead and do what is needed. As we saw with Lewis, the guiding hand of providence does not eliminate the need for human response and ingenuity but in fact calls for both. It is *because* there is a design and purpose that Frodo can have hope, and so use all his own resources to accomplish the task at hand.

As the story develops, the great elf lord, Elrond, speaks to all those gathered together with him in council and sums up the situation:

That is the purpose for which you are called hither. Called, I say, though I have not called you to me, strangers from distant lands. You have come here and are here met, in the very nick of time, by chance as it may seem. Yet it is not so. Believe rather that it is so ordered that we, who sit here,

[8] Tolkien, *The Fellowship of the Ring*, 87.

and none others, must now find counsel for the peril of the world.[9]

Elrond is clear: he is not the guiding hand. He did not call them together. This is not a plot arranged by human beings (or elves). But he rejects the idea that it is all chance. No, "it is so ordered" that this small group together should decide the fate of the world. And it is the recognition of this providential guiding hand that gives them heart to attempt what seems like a hopeless quest.

As it turns out, Frodo and his companions have to use *all* their strength and heart and wits to accomplish the quest. They are called to personal bravery and heroism beyond anything they could have imagined. Still, without the constant hand of providence throughout the story, the quest would never have been fulfilled. Time and again, help is supplied along the way; resources are provided just at the right time and betrayals turn out to their advantage. But Frodo, Gandalf, and the others are not puppets, yanked this way and that by the all-powerful hand of fate. Rather, they are fully free actors, choosing to give themselves to the task and cooperate with the hidden hand of providence guiding the story.

To say this differently: the reader of *The Lord of the Rings* is left in no doubt that there is a providential hand at work *in the story*; there is a purpose and a guiding hand that, through the actions of the main characters, will bring things to a good ending. This is why both the characters in the story and the readers of the story carry on with

---

[9] Tolkien, *The Fellowship of the Ring*, 291.

hope for a good outcome. There is, of course, genuine tragedy and loss, but we as readers know that the story will somehow turn out well. What is good and true and beautiful will prevail, even amidst much loss.

In a personal letter, Tolkien himself describes how he incorporated references to God and divine providence in *The Lord of the Rings*:

> I have purposely kept all allusions to the highest matters down to mere hints, perceptible only by the most attentive, or kept them under unexplained symbolic forms. So God and the "angelic" god, the Lords or powers of the West, only peep through in such places as Gandalf's conversation with Frodo . . . or in Faramir's Númenórean grace at dinner.[10]

A Game of Thrones. When we turn to the fantasy world created by George Martin, *A Game of Thrones*, the contrast could hardly be more stark. Martin slowly and artfully introduces the reader to a vast array of characters and lands, with a long and complex back-history that the reader only gradually comes to learn. As a reader, however, I quickly came to the conclusion that there is no sense of

---

[10] J. R. R. Tolkien, "Letter to Robert Murray" (November 4, 1954), in Humphrey Carpenter, ed., *The Letters of J. R. R. Tolkien* (Boston: Houghton Mifflin, 1981), 201. As Tolkien observes later in this same letter, the one brief reference to prayer (and so to God) in the Trilogy occurs when Faramir is hosting Frodo and Sam in the hidden cave. While references to God are few and indirect in *The Lord of the Rings*, Tolkien's wider mythology as found in *The Silmarillion* speaks directly of God and presents God as an actor in the stories.

a guiding hand of providence *acting within the story*. Martin's fictional world is full of references to the gods and to temples, but most of the characters seem to doubt that the gods are there to hear or help, and as readers we do not take the gods seriously as actors in the tale. To state the contrast plainly: Tolkien makes almost no reference in his story to God or to the gods, but the hand of divine providence is everywhere at work. Martin makes constant references to the gods and his characters continually appeal to them, but there is virtually no sense of divine providence at work in his world. Rather, it is a world of power, lust, envy, bloodshed, and the constant maneuvering for ascendancy. There is no providential sense of a greater purpose or goal: we are just given an epic tale of individuals and families vying with one another—and mostly killing one another—for survival, power, and dominance. In the words of Queen Cersei, "When you play the game of thrones, you win or you die. There is no middle ground."[11]

There are, for sure, characters who show nobility and a sense of justice, and the audience identifies with them and wishes for their success. But they are few and there is no sense that the author is committed to them or that a hand of providence guides them. The underlying principle of this fantasy world is neatly stated in a short back-and-forth between two of the more likable characters. At one point the young girl Arya complains, "It's not fair." Her wise half-brother Jon responds, "Nothing is fair."[12] Where

---

[11] George R. R. Martin, *A Game of Thrones* (New York: Bantam Books, 2011), 488.

[12] Martin, *A Game of Thrones*, 75.

there is no conviction that justice will prevail, at least in an ultimate way, there is no hope. If, in the end, those who show mercy and justice prevail in "the game of thrones," it will not be due to the fact that Martin's world is somehow good and ordered by a divine, providential hand. It will happen because the human author arbitrarily decided to make things turn out that way.

Notably, what George Martin says about himself and the world he created confirms the reader's sense of the *absence* of providence and hope in his fantasy world. In a personal interview, Martin expresses his great admiration for Tolkien and acknowledges the debt that he owes him. He speaks with admiration for the realism and even tragedy that he finds in Tolkien's great epic. But then the crucial difference emerges. Tolkien was a faithful Catholic all his life, and his faith in God shaped the way he wrote his stories.[13] Martin describes himself as a lapsed Catholic, as an atheist or agnostic. "I find religion and spirituality fascinating. I would like to believe this isn't the end and there's something more, but I can't convince the rational part of me that that makes any sense whatsoever." As for God or the gods, "I've never been satisfied by any of the answers that are given. If there really is a benevolent, loving God, why is the world full of rape and torture? Why do we even have pain?" Instead, Martin aims to create a world of "realism." He says, "I think

---

[13] Tolkien identifies his Christian faith as one of the most important biographical details that has impacted the shape of his epic tale: "More important, I am a Christian (which can be deduced from my stories), and in fact a Roman Catholic." "Letter to Deborah Webster" (October 25, 1958), in Carpenter, *The Letters of J. R. R. Tolkien*, 288.

the books are realistic. I've always liked grey characters."[14] And this is just what we find in *A Game of Thrones*. There are shards of light and virtue but violence, brutality, and dishonesty dominate the narrative and its characters. It is a world seemingly without the hand of divine providence and, as such, a world without hope and ultimate meaning. Anything can and might happen; it all seems to depend on the whim and fancy of the human author.

PROVIDENCE IN THE BIBLICAL STORY

When we turn to the biblical story, the guiding hand of a providential God is there right from the beginning. The world and all its inhabitants are created directly by God through his Word. They are declared as being "good" from the start. The tempter enters the scene and, in short order, our first parents fall prey to the seduction. Evil enters the world and the purpose of God is marred. Yet even here, the presence and purpose of God is evident. The Lord God seeks out Adam and Eve, finds them, and speaks with them even when they try to hide in their shame and sin. He announces the dire consequences of their sin, but speaks in veiled language of ultimate victory: "I will put enmity between you and the woman, and between your seed and her seed; he shall bruise your head, and you shall bruise his heel" (Gen 3:15, RSVCE).

Time and again, the Lord God acts to bring the human race back to himself. Through Noah, Abraham, Moses, and David, he establishes a succession of covenants

---

[14] James Hibberd, "A Dance with Dragons Interview," interview with George R. R. Martin, July 12, 2011, http://ew.com/article/2011/07/12/george-martin-talks-a-dance-with-dragons.

that, by stages, prepare the way for the complete recovery of the human race from its fall. Through the prophets he tirelessly calls his people back. And finally, in the decisive event, God sends the angel Gabriel to a virgin daughter of Israel. In Mary's consent to his plan, the Word is made flesh and the undoing of the exile is begun.

In the story of the Gospels, we read how Jesus of Nazareth ushers in the kingdom of God through his preaching, teaching, healing, and calling. Then, in the event that appears to signal the utter failure of his mission, Jesus dies upon a cross. But he knew—and as enlightened readers of the Gospels, we know—that this "failure" is precisely the providential act that delivers us from our sin and from the power of the devil. In the divine narrative of the Gospel, betrayal, abandonment, and death paradoxically lead to victory.

The adventure of the Gospel, however, does not end with the Resurrection of Jesus from the dead and his Ascension. The story continues, the Spirit is poured out in power, and the battle for the human race becomes even more intense. The Book of Revelation in particular displays this ongoing battle in graphic imagery and powerful visions. Things often look very bad for the followers of the Lamb, but appearances are misleading. Jesus now reigns as the one who has authority over human history, and he will bring the story to a glorious finale when all our enemies will finally be overcome and we will dwell with God forever. God himself will dwell with us, and there will be no more tears or mourning or pain or death (Rev 21:3-4). What was lost will be found again, but the end result will be even more glorious than the beginning. *This* is the great adventure of the Gospel, and it reveals a provident God who patiently brings about his purposes by acting in, with, and through the free choices of his characters.

PROVIDENCE AND THE VIRTUE OF HOPE

The premise of this book is that each of us has been born into a great adventure—the adventure of the Gospel of Christ—and we can learn something of how to make our way through this adventure by pondering the "adventures" that we imagine and create. By viewing the hand of providence and hope in stories such as *The Horse and His Boy* and *The Lord of the Rings*, in contrast with the lack of providence and hope in *A Game of Thrones*, we can glean some insight into how providence functions in the costly adventure of the Gospel.

To conclude this chapter, I want to give specific attention to the realities of providence, hope, and the gift of the Spirit, in order to help us navigate our way through the adventure set before us. And for this task we will have recourse to the Catechism. The Catechism opens its treatment of providence by teaching that "the universe was created 'in a state of journeying' (*in statu viae*) toward an ultimate perfection yet to be attained, to which God has destined it. We call 'divine providence' the dispositions by which God guides his creation toward this perfection" (CCC 302). This "state of journeying" is the stage that provides the space for our activity in history—this is the costly adventure of the Gospel. As we have seen in our examples of providence in literature and film, the providential hand that guides the story does not eliminate the free choices of the characters but works with them to accomplish and fulfill the story. This co-working is beautifully described in the Catechism:

> God is the sovereign master of his plan. But to carry it out he also makes use of his creatures' cooperation. This use is not a sign of weakness, but rather a token of almighty God's greatness and goodness. For God grants his creatures not only their existence, but also the dignity of acting on their own, of being causes and principles for each other, and thus of cooperating in the accomplishment of his plan. (306)

Crucially, we do not usually see how things are going to work out. We cooperate with God's plan, we live and act in hope, but we cannot peer around the corner and perceive how things will turn out. What we find in all great adventures is also true for us. The Catechism, again, states,

> We firmly believe that God is master of the world and of its history. But the ways of his providence are often unknown to us. Only at the end, when our partial knowledge ceases, when we see God "face to face" [1 Cor 13:12], will we fully know the ways by which—even through the dramas of evil and sin—God has guided his creation to that definitive sabbath rest [cf. Gen 2:2] for which he created heaven and earth. (314)

Notice the language here of "dramas." This is what we are seeking to capture when we speak of "the great and costly adventure of the Gospel": it is the outworking of the dramas of sin and grace, through the free activity of human beings like ourselves, that God brings his plan to completion.

How do we find our way along the paths of this great drama, this costly adventure, to which we have been called? To quote the Apostle Paul, *we live by hope, not by sight*: "But hope that is seen is not hope. For who hopes for what he sees? But if we hope for what we do not see, we wait for it with perseverance" (Rom 8:24–25). It is the theological virtue of hope that carries us through. "Hope is the theological virtue by which we desire the kingdom of heaven and eternal life as our happiness, placing our trust in Christ's promises and relying not on our own strength, but on the help of the grace of the Holy Spirit" (CCC 1817). Notice the orientation of hope to eternal life: through hope we trust not in ourselves or what we see in the world, but in the promises of Christ. The Catechism further speaks about hope in terms of what it accomplishes in us as we journey through life: "It keeps man from discouragement; it sustains him during times of abandonment; it opens up his heart in expectation of eternal beatitude" (1818). It is hope that buoys us up and enables us to persevere through trials, hardships, perplexity, and setbacks.

In my view there is no better contemporary description of the virtue of hope than Josef Pieper's short treatment.[15] Pieper underlines the specific *supernatural hope*

---

[15] Pieper, *Faith, Hope, Love*. Pieper's discussion of hope is dense but brimming with penetrating insight and inspiration.

that we have through Christ: "Christ is . . . the actual fulfillment of our hope. . . . This inherent linking of our hope to Christ is so crucial that one who is not in Christ has no hope."[16] But with great insight he describes how "natural hope" (that is, hope for things in this life) is ultimately anchored in and strengthened by supernatural hope: "Supernatural hope, then . . . is able to rejuvenate and give new vigor even to natural hope."[17] What he means by this is that as our hope in Christ and eternal life is strengthened, so our hope for things in this world is also rejuvenated. This is paradoxical: you might expect that those who hope in eternal life would *not* have much hope for things in this life. But the opposite is the case. Those who hope in Christ for eternal life also typically have more hope *for this life* than those who do not know Christ, despite the insecurity and uncertainty of things in the world as we know it.

> In the most literal sense of these words, nothing more eminently preserves and founds "eternal youth" than the theological virtue of hope. It alone can bestow on man the certain possession of that aspiration that is at once relaxed and disciplined, that adaptability and readiness, that strong-hearted freshness, that resilient joy, that steady perseverance in trust that so distinguish the young and make them so lovable.[18]

[16] Pieper, *Faith, Hope, Love*, 106.
[17] Pieper, *Faith, Hope, Love*, 109–10.
[18] Pieper, *Faith, Hope, Love*, 110–11.

PROVIDENCE, HOPE, AND THE GIFT OF THE SPIRIT

As our hope in Christ deepens, our hope for the world also increases. It is precisely because the source of our hope is not *in* this world, but *in* Christ, that we can have hope *for* this world.

Pieper also shows how hope is distinguished from both despair (its opposite) and presumption (its counterfeit). Earlier, we noted the heavy burden of *acedia* and despair that afflicts our culture today. The true antidote to despair is not positive thinking or a bright smile, but the real activity of hope and the joy of the Lord in our hearts.

> *Acedia* is a kind of sadness . . . more specifically, a sadness in view of the divine good in man. This sadness because of the God-given ennobling of human nature causes inactivity, depression, discouragement. . . . The opposite of *acedia* is not industry and diligence, but magnanimity and that joy which is a fruit of the supernatural love of God.[19]

Let's be clear: the hope we are talking about here is not confidence that everything in this life will turn out supremely well; it is not an optimistic view of the world or of human nature. Instead, it is the knowledge of our being known and loved by God and called to eternal life, and it produces in us joy and energy for living and acting in this world in order to see God's purposes come to pass.

How many of us lack hope and expectation for our lives? We may believe in God but our active hope for eter-

---

[19] Pieper, *Faith, Hope, Love*, 118.

nal life may be quite dim. And our engagement with the adventure of our lives, day by day, may be weak or tepid. A living faith awakens us to our true destiny and calling. And a living hope energizes us to face the uncertainty of life, not with fear and despair, but with an adventurous spirit because we know that God is with us. Following the counsel of the Apostle Peter, we are called to *set our hope fully on the grace that is coming to us* (1 Pet 1:13). This is a choice: this involves *acting* in hope because God is with us, he has a purpose for us, and he has given us his Spirit.

THE GIFT OF THE SPIRIT

To conclude, we should speak briefly about the person of the Holy Spirit. Christ calls the Spirit "another counselor" and promises that he would be with us (and in us) always (John 14:17, 26). To accompany us on our way, God has given us his Spirit—as Christians *we actually have God the Holy Spirit dwelling in us.* This is the best of all possible companions. In Paul's words, when we become Christians we receive the Spirit of adoption who speaks to us from within, revealing to us that we really are children of God who can have hope (Rom 8:15–17). Who are we really? We are sons and daughters of God. And we have a Father who never fails and never grows weary. One of the main works of the Spirit is to reveal to us that God is our true Father. The Spirit bears witness within that we are truly children of God (Rom 8:15–16).

Earlier in this chapter we looked at the figure of Shasta in *The Horse and His Boy*, to see an example of providence at work. But now we can draw something further from this story. Shasta not only experienced the hand of providence in his life through the figure of Aslan. This fatherless boy came to know that he had a father and that he was in fact the crown prince of the kingdom. He was Cor, Prince of Archenland. The great joy and satisfaction that we find in this story does not arise just from the fact that Shasta escapes servitude and proves himself the hero. Our greatest delight, perhaps, is that an orphan who had no hope in the world discovers that he is a prince, with a father, a brother, and a host of companions and friends. He is given an identity from which to carry on the adventure of his life. Isn't this a parable about each of us?

Just consider your situation in Christ. You have God, the Lord of all, as your Father. You are joined to Christ and his people and nothing can separate you from the love of Christ (Rom 8:35). And you have the Spirit as your companion and guide, revealing truth to you, correcting you, and helping you in your weakness. You and I have every reason to trust in the providential hand of our Father, as we live by hope and walk with the companionship of the Spirit. We don't need to shrink back in fear or drug ourselves into senselessness because of despair. Is life complex, confusing, perplexing, and full of uncertainty? Of course it is—what kind of adventure would it be without these things? But we are not orphans. We are not alone in the universe. There is a providential justice and mercy at work in the world, and we have tasted and seen something of it. Strengthened by grace we can press on in hope in this costly adventure of discipleship.

* *Portrait* *
RUTH

Ruth is one of the most remarkable figures in the Old Testament. She was not a daughter of Israel—she was a foreigner, a woman of the land of Moab. As the story opens, we hear that an Israelite family (Naomi, her husband, and two sons) fled to Moab because of a famine in Israel. The husband then died and the two sons married two Moabite women (one being Ruth). Then the two sons also died, leaving Naomi alone with her two daughters-in-law. At this point, Naomi decides to return to the land of Israel, and she entreats both of the young women to leave her and return to their fathers' homes in Moab. Naomi is beaten down through her misfortune because the hand of the Lord has been against her (Ruth 1:13), and says in effect that there is no *hope* for either of them ever finding another husband if they stay with her.

Weeping, the first daughter-in-law departs, but Ruth clings to Naomi and refuses to leave, uttering the renowned words of loyalty and faithfulness: "Where you go, I will go; where you lodge, I will lodge; your people shall be my people, and your God my God. Where you die, I will die—there will I be buried" (Ruth 1:16–17, NRSVCE). Ruth, in fact, acts in hope. Despite the dire circumstances, she remains true to Naomi and carries on in hope for a good outcome for both of them.

And this is just what happens. Through Ruth's bold initiative, Naomi's clever advice, and Boaz's keen sense of justice, Ruth becomes the wife of Boaz and bears a son. Naomi, who had declared herself bitter and cast off, is now declared blessed by those around her: "Blessed be the LORD, who has not left you this day without next-of-kin; and may his name be renowned in Israel" (Ruth 4:14, NRSVCE). Strengthened by hope, Ruth remained faithful, enabling the blessing of the Lord to come upon Naomi and herself. Even more, she became, through the providence of God, the great-grandmother of King David and so was enrolled in the lineage of Christ Jesus (Matt 1:5).

·❖·

CHAPTER SIX

TRIALS AND SUFFERING IN THE COSTLY
ADVENTURE OF DISCIPLESHIP

My child, when you come to serve the Lord, prepare yourself for testing.

—Sirach 2:1 (NRSVCE)

Blessed are you when they insult you and perse-
cute you and speak every evil against you falsely
because of me. Rejoice and be glad, for your reward is great in heaven. For thus they persecuted
the prophets who came before you.

—Matt 5:11–12

For he is a chosen vessel of mine to carry my name
before the Gentiles and kings and the people of
Israel. For I will show him how much he must
suffer for the sake of my name.

—Acts 9:15–16

WE now return to the *costly* part of adventure. Earlier we examined the cost of becoming disciples, of giving our lives away to the Lord Jesus. This is the *active* cost that we are called to embrace. In this chapter we are looking especially at the *passive* or *receptive* part of the cost. How do we handle setbacks and loss when we had such hopes for things turning out well? What do we do when suffering comes our way? Why does evil seem to strike at us so unexpectedly and without rhyme or reason?

For me, embracing the *active cost* of discipleship, difficult though it is, seems easier than handling the suffering and grief that breaks into my life like a sudden thunderstorm. Despite the advance warning that such trials will befall us—Jesus tells his disciples that they will endure suffering for his sake—I am still surprised when they appear and I find that I need *great grace* to come through well. But we also quickly discover that we are not immune from the sufferings that befall *all* people, whether Christians or not. The hurricanes that blow and the cancers that devour appear in our lives just as they do in others'. What do we make of all this? How do we come through, not just barely surviving, but thriving in faith, hope, and love?

The answer to this question is many-sided and occupies the final three chapters of the book. In this present chapter I want to focus primarily on how we handle trials and suffering. How can we prepare ourselves for this in Christ? What are the qualities and virtues needed to embrace this suffering and bear much fruit for the Lord? And can we gain insight and inspiration from the adventures that we love, so that we are better equipped to glorify God in our trials and suffering?

A disclaimer: human suffering, and especially suffering endured "in Christ," is a deep mystery, far beyond my ability to plumb. The griefs that Christ bore for us, the sorrows that Mary endured, the dark night described by St. John of the Cross, these are all beyond our capability to fathom. We cannot hope to touch bottom here. But if we cannot reach the bottom, perhaps we can at least *wade* into this topic and be strengthened and equipped to bear our suffering with understanding, holiness, and joy. We can prepare for adventures, but only in the moment of the actual adventure can we act and receive the help we need. So it is with trial and suffering: we can be prepared and equipped so that it does not catch us by surprise, but only in the moment of the trial and suffering can we receive divine help to endure and persevere to the glory of God.

ADVERSITY IN TRUE ADVENTURE

Can you think of an adventure worth its salt that does not include trials, difficulties, perplexity, and even suffering? If these are lacking, where is the interest? Where is the drama? What is the value? Bland, predictable stories where nothing is risked and nothing is at stake simply do not capture our attention. Consider some of the most popular adventure stories in the past generation. If Luke Skywalker had been left in peace, living with his aunt and uncle on their insignificant planet, he would be of no interest to anyone. If Harry Potter had remained undetected, dwelling in the closet under the stairs, no one in his world (or ours) would know or care about his life. If Katniss Everdeen had not volunteered to replace her sister in the Hunger Games, she would not have become the spark of revolution in her own world (or the captivating figure in ours). Without the intense tests and trials set before these young heroes, none of them would have become the iconic figures of the past generation. But each of them was *chosen* and thrown into an adventure that was chock full of trials, setbacks, perplexities, and personal suffering. It is precisely because of this that they—and the adventures that surround them—are so captivating and compelling to millions of fans.

Why has a generation of moviegoers been so fascinated with *Mission Impossible* and the Jason Bourne tales? Yes, they are well produced and heart-pounding; but even more, we are drawn into the drama of the main characters: Will they survive the attempts to kill them? Can they overcome the cleverness and technical resources of their opponents? Will they be able to use their physical skills and their wits to overcome and triumph? We seem never to tire of this kind of adventure, and the fact that the characters face serious trials and difficulties makes them *more* attractive, not less. Have you ever heard anyone say, "I really like these stories but I'd like it much better if the main characters were never placed in danger or faced with any real challenges or sufferings to overcome"? No, we are drawn to these adventures and get involved with them *because* there is something at stake that is worth suffering and even dying for.

This quality of the adventures that we love and to which we are magnetically drawn tells us something important about the real world we live in and about our own lives. There *is* something enormously important—something at stake—in the world, and by extension, something deeply significant about our own lives. There *is* something worth suffering for and even dying for. It makes a difference whether we "triumph" and "conquer." Peering more deeply, these adventures that we love can help us see that there is a fundamental "battle" or "struggle" going on in the world and in each of our lives. Life is not just about getting along, putting food on the table, and having fun. There is a war going on, there is evil seeking to triumph, and we have to be ready to pour out our lives to help defeat this evil and win the battle.

I hope you can see where this is leading. When the First Letter of John says, "The Son of God appeared for this reason, to destroy the works of the devil" (1 John 3:8), it is pointing to a fundamental battle that lies at the core of the Gospel. The infant Jesus was not allowed time to grow up in quiet and calm, but a storm broke upon him and only through the revelation of an angel was he able to flee and avoid destruction from his enemies (Matt 2:13–18). We are told that the "dragon" in the book of Revelation (who is Satan), when he failed to destroy Jesus, went to make war against his faithful people (Rev 12:17). That's us. We were born into a battle, born behind enemy lines, and we cannot make sense of our lives apart from this context of struggle. We know by revelation that our battle is not against human enemies, but against the spiritual powers of darkness (Eph 6:12)—but it is a battle nonetheless.

Here, I believe, we run up against a paradox. On the one hand, we are transfixed by great adventure stories where the fate of the world hangs in a balance and where the main characters are asked to pour out their lives and to struggle even to death for the sake of saving the world. On the other hand, we try to set up our *own* lives in a way that maximizes security, predictability, safety, and freedom from every form of suffering. We put together an itinerary for ourselves that avoids the very things that make great adventures significant and attractive. The point, of course, is not to dash out seeking hardships and trials; the goal is not to suffer as much as possible. Rather, we are called to seek the truth adventurously, to pursue what is right and good, to stand against those who do evil, and to ready ourselves to endure and embrace the trials and suffering that we know will come.

The adventure stories that we read and watch can function in two very different ways. For some people, they provide a kind of *substitute* or *proxy* for adventure in their own lives. Instead of walking out and facing the dragons of our day, they stay at home in their safe havens and read about the dragon-tales of imaginative characters. Watching becomes a substitute for doing. We become impotent in action and unable to experience the real thing. This is a real danger in our time.

But for others, the adventures they watch and read give them a "shot in the arm" to go out and face the real adventure of their own lives. Tales of dragons and wizards provide an imaginative lens through which they can grasp and engage the battles that they must face. These adventures can shape and nourish the virtuous life and instill a desire to conduct ourselves nobly and with honor. This is true preeminently of the testimony of the saints and martyrs. We read (and watch) dramatic narratives of their lives *so that* we might be inspired to go and do likewise, with the help of God.

To illustrate the role of trials, testing, and suffering, I offer two examples from fictional stories, the first from the Chronicles of Narnia by C. S. Lewis and the second from *The Lord of the Rings* by J. R. R. Tolkien.

TESTING AND TRIALS IN *THE SILVER CHAIR*

In C. S. Lewis's story *The Silver Chair*, the Christ-figure, Aslan, commissions two young children to undertake a specific task with clearly-stated goals and predicted sign-posts along the way. Speaking to Jill Pole, the great Lion gives this charge: "And now hear your task. . . . I lay on you this command, that you seek this lost prince until either you have found him and brought him to his father's house, or else died in the attempt, or else gone back into your own world."[1] Jill is then required to memorize four "signs" that will occur along the path of this quest, and Aslan is insistent that she review them and repeat them. Finally, Aslan cautions Jill solemnly, that she will find things much harder going once she lands in Narnia:

> I give you a warning. Here on the mountain I have spoken to you clearly: I will not often do so down in Narnia. Here on the mountain, the air is clear and your mind is clear; as you drop down into Narnia, the air will thicken. Take great care that it does not confuse your mind. And the signs which you have learned here will not look at all as you expect

[1]   C. S. Lewis, *The Silver Chair* (New York: HarperCollins, 1981), 24.

them to look, when you meet them there. . . . Remember the signs and believe the signs.[2]

Sure enough, because of pride, inattentiveness, and the hardships of the road, Jill and Eustace botch the first three signs. And they know it: they are aware of their failure and bemoan their weaknesses and faults. Nonetheless, through a providential hand guiding them and the steady influence of their companion, Puddleglum, they get back on the right road and, in the end, fulfill the task given to them.

C. S. Lewis sets up the story beautifully. The "test" is clearly set out with a warning that it will be difficult to stay on the right path. Despite their periodic efforts, the children succumb to the trials that befall them. In one sense, they fail the test miserably. But in another sense, with the help of providence and a readiness to acknowledge their faults and return to the task, they eventually succeed. In the end, they don't receive from Aslan the resounding praise, "Well done, good and faithful servants," but they still get a commendation for having done what they were asked to do. When Jill is about to apologize for their failures, Aslan interrupts her with these words: "Think of that no more. I will not always be scolding. You have done the work for which I sent you into Narnia."[3]

Both Jill and Eustace show moments of courage and cleverness that get them out of scrapes along the way. But the real hero of the tale is the ever-pessimistic Puddleglum. He is the one who rouses them in the Giants' city to

[2] C. S. Lewis, *The Silver Chair*, 26–27.
[3] C. S. Lewis, *The Silver Chair*, 260.

play their part with courage and make their escape. He is the one who encourages them when they are tempted to despair, insisting that the words of Aslan will be fulfilled. This prompts Jill to praise him for his courage: "You talk as if you were afraid of everything, when you're really as brave as—as a lion."[4] And in the climactic moment of the story, it is Puddleglum who saves the day: The witch has cast a spell over them through a magical green powder burning in the fire. Jill makes one valiant attempt to call them all back, but the power of the spell is too great. Then with great effort, Puddleglum rouses himself and does violence to his own flesh in order to break the bondage:

> But Puddleglum, desperately gathering all his strength, walked over to the fire. Then he did a very brave thing. He knew it wouldn't hurt him quite as much as it would hurt a human. . . . But he knew it would hurt him badly enough; and so it did. With his bare feet he stamped on the fire, grinding a large part of it into ashes on the flat hearth.[5]

To defeat the witch, one of the characters had to step forward and embrace suffering. Puddleglum was ready at the critical moment to do violence to himself for the greater good. This is not only a marvelous parable of how to do violence to oneself in order to avoid the enchantment of sin. It also displays how the great deeds of the world only come about through testing and suffering.

---

4   Lewis, *The Silver Chair*, 255.
5   Lewis, *The Silver Chair*, 195.

The Silver Chair offers a simple but powerful portrayal of the tests, trials, and sufferings that are required to overcome evil and accomplish great things. But there is gritty reality in the story as well. The children actually don't follow the signs (except the last one). Their pettiness, quarreling, and love of comfort cause them to miss the cues they were meant to follow. The good news is that the quest succeeds despite these failures, and they are enabled to play a real and significant role in bringing about the deliverance of the prince. Aslan was able to use them even in their weakness.

This is good news for us. We, too, sometimes receive a clear word and call from God. But what appears obvious "on the mountain" gets fogged-over down in the messy realities of life. We, too, are tested, to see if we will follow the word of the Lord and press on despite difficulties and setbacks: "Blessed is the man who endures testing, for when he has stood the test he will receive the crown of life which is promised to those who love him" (Jas 1:12). We can be grateful that the outcomes of our lives do not depend on our flawless performance. As we persevere, God our Father will bring us through, despite setbacks and failures, and enable us to be genuine co-workers with him in the mission of the kingdom of God.

FRODO BAGGINS AND THE
EXPERIENCE OF DEEP SUFFERING

C. S. Lewis portrays the experience of testing and trials in *The Silver Chair* in a somewhat lighthearted way, suitable for children. But there is nothing lighthearted about the kind of suffering that Frodo Baggins is invited to embrace in *The Lord of the Rings*. Though the story begins light-heartedly, by the second chapter things have become serious and even grim as Gandalf lays out for Frodo the full import of what lies before him. Frodo's initial response is predictable: he is terrified by the news that he possesses *the* great Ring of the Dark Lord, Sauron, who is seeking him even as they speak. In a show of remarkable courage and wisdom that surprises even Gandalf, Frodo accepts his role and agrees to bear the Ring out of the Shire:

> As far as I understand what you have said, I suppose I must keep the Ring and guard it, at least for the present, whatever it may do to me. . . . But this would mean exile, a flight from danger into danger, drawing it after me. And I suppose I must go alone, if I am to do that and save the Shire. But I feel very small, and very uprooted, and well—desperate. The Enemy is so strong and terrible.[6]

And so he sets out, pursued by Dark Riders whose presence (and voice) freezes the blood with fear. Aided along the way by a myriad of helpers (Sam, Merry, and Pippin, Gildor and the Elves, Farmer Maggot, Tom Bombadil, Glorfindel, and, most of all, Aragorn), Frodo barely makes it to the safety of Rivendell. But now he has faced the terror of the Riders and been stabbed with an evil blade that nearly turns him into a wraith. Now he now understands just how evil and powerful his foes are.

A council is held and the conclusion is reached that

---

[6] Tolkien, *The Fellowship of the Ring*, 88–89.

the Ring must be carried to the land of the Dark Lord and cast into the mountain of fire. Bilbo pipes up and asks the question on everyone's mind: Who will take the Ring to the fire? Silence falls. Finally Frodo speaks. In words that seal his fate and show his great courage, he says: "I will take the Ring, though I do not know the way."[7] And so the great quest of the Nine Walkers (the Fellowship of the Ring) begins. Along the way, each of the Company is faced with trials specific to them and must show courage and loyalty to win through. Frodo, too, has his share of trials, but his real test begins when Boromir attempts to seize the Ring and the Fellowship is dispersed. Though he sets out to fulfill the quest alone, Sam, his trusted companion, catches up with him and accompanies his master on the final stage of the quest.

The chapters that narrate the journey of Frodo and Sam to the mountain of fire are magnificent but they make for painful reading. Tolkien paints scenes of blackness, misery, torture, and pain almost beyond imagining. It's all that Frodo can do to put one foot in front of the next. He is in constant agony, hopeless of ever reaching the mountain, aware that even if he does he will never live through the aftermath. But he plods onward, strengthened outwardly by Sam's constant help and inwardly by the miraculous vigor granted through the waybread of the Elves. Against all hope and odds, the quest is accomplished and the Dark Lord is utterly overthrown. In one sense, Frodo fails at the end—he gives way to the power of the Ring and cannot resist the temptation to take the Ring for him-

---

[7] Tolkien, *The Fellowship of the Ring*, 324.

self. He *cannot* destroy it. But somehow providentially, this very inability was foreseen—no one could have accomplished this quest on his own strength. And so Gollum plays his role, seizing the Ring for himself and then falling into the abyss along with the Ring. Frodo is rightly showered with the greatest honors for bearing the Ring—he did everything that was in him to do.[8] But the horrendous suffering he experienced has ongoing consequences that make it impossible for him to return to "normal" life. Pain and distress mark his next few years, and a way is arranged for Frodo to leave Middle-earth and travel to the Undying Lands of the Elves for the healing that he needs.

What is the reader to make of this powerful account of deep suffering? Tolkien is insistent that *The Lord of the Rings* is not an allegory of the Christian life or of anything else. But he recognizes that the truths of the Christian faith shaped how he wrote the story, and he readily acknowledges that readers are justified in seeing spiritual truths exemplified in the story.[9] Many have

[8] In a letter to an inquirer, Tolkien speaks of "sacrificial situations" where "the good of the world depends on the behaviour of an individual in circumstances which demand of him suffering and endurance far beyond the normal—even, it may happen ... demand a strength of body and mind which he does not possess: he is in a sense doomed to failure, doomed to fall to temptation or be broken by pressure against his will.... Frodo was in such a position." But Tolkien adds that Frodo "was very justly accorded the highest honors." Carpenter, *Letters of J. R. R. Tolkien*, 233, 234. In a separate letter, Tolkien says that "I do not think that Frodo's was a *moral* failure. ... Frodo had done what he could and spent himself completely (as an instrument of Providence) and had produced a situation in which the object of his quest could be achieved." Ibid., 326.

[9] Tolkien writes, "Something of the teller's own reflections and values will inevitably get worked in. This is not the same as allegory. We all,

seen in Frodo's burden of bearing the Ring a reflection of Christ carrying the Cross and bearing the sorrowful burden of our sin. The miraculous power of the Elves' bread has been likened to the spiritual power of the Eucharist, especially for strengthening the faithful in times of great trial and suffering. In fact, the trials and tests of *all* the main characters offer profound examples that can instruct and inspire the reader.

One profound truth, not typically noted, is the presence of "grace" in the story of Frodo and the Ring: grace that comes sometimes directly from on high and grace that is often mediated through the help of others. Frodo is tempted to think that he must bear this burden alone and go off in the wilderness by himself. Instead, he is "given" wonderful companions and a host of helpers along the way, without which he would never have come close to escaping the Black Riders. Then again, when fleeing the Company, he sets out by himself to carry the Ring to the fire. But this instinct to go alone is again frustrated. Sam catches up and accompanies him to the finish; Gollum tracks him down and proves to be the irreplaceable guide; Faramir and his men re-provision them for the journey; the phial of Galadriel delivers them from the power of Shelob; the waybread of the Elves keeps them on their feet; the infighting among the Orcs allows them to escape and flee; the bold maneuvers by the captains of the West keep the Eye of Sauron distracted; and a divine-like urgency and strength inspires them for the last lap up the mountain.

in groups or as individuals, *exemplify* general principles; but we do not *represent* them." Carpenter, *The Letters of J. R. R. Tolkien*, 233.

In the end the most decrepit and pitiable of all creatures, Gollum, enables the quest to be finally accomplished.

The story of Frodo and the Ring is preeminently a story of grace, of help in time of need, and of the turning of evil to good. Frodo suffers intensely and has to bear his part of the quest alone, though even here Sam bears the Ring for a short time and carries Frodo himself with the Ring at the crisis point. But Frodo was not allowed to "go it alone" in the quest; he was accompanied in his trials and suffering by extraordinary grace and help at every turn. His intense suffering was personal and unique to him, but not solitary; he accomplished the quest but only with a plenitude of grace.[10]

TRIALS, TESTING, AND SUFFERING IN DISCIPLESHIP

We should not be surprised by the trials and tests that come our way as followers of Christ. After all, if Christ himself had to undergo trials and suffering, why would we think to avoid them? If we are those who follow the Lamb wherever he goes (Rev 14:4), then we should expect to share in his afflictions.

What happened immediately after the baptism of Jesus? Luke says that Jesus, who was full of the Holy Spirit,

---

[10] When speaking of Gollum's role in the destruction of the Ring, Tolkien himself uses the word "grace" to describe how Frodo's pity was turned to a good end. "But at this point, the 'salvation' of the world and Frodo's own 'salvation' is achieved by his previous *pity* and forgiveness of injury. . . . [Gollum] did rob him and injure him in the end—but by a 'grace', that last betrayal was at a precise juncture when the final evil deed was the most beneficial thing anyone could have done for Frodo!" Carpenter, *The Letters of J. R. R. Tolkien*, 234.

was led *by the Spirit* out into the wilderness for forty days, to be tested by the devil (Luke 4:1–2). The *first* thing Jesus had to do after his anointing for his saving mission was to go out and withstand the temptation of the devil. And the Holy Spirit *led* Jesus into this testing. Again, as Jesus faced gruesome death on a cross, he prayed to his Father three times, asking that this suffering might be lifted, but he resolved to follow his Father's will and endure the Cross for our sake. Referring to Jesus's prayer in Gethsemane, the Letter to the Hebrews tells us that Jesus offered up prayers and petitions "with loud cries and tears" to his Father who was able to save him from death, and that his Father heard his prayer. Though he was the Father's perfect Son, yet he still "learned obedience" through the things that he suffered (Heb 5:7–8). Jesus himself, as the new and second Adam, endured tests, trials, and the most profound suffering. Where Adam failed to stand, Jesus was the victor.

On many occasions, Jesus signals that a crucial part of being his disciple is the readiness to suffer for his sake. When teaching the Beatitudes, Jesus ends by pointing to the suffering and persecution that his disciples will encounter:

> Blessed are those who are persecuted for righteousness' sake, for theirs is the kingdom of heaven. Blessed are you when others revile you and persecute you and utter all kinds of evil against you falsely on my account. Rejoice and be glad, for your reward is great in heaven. (Matt 5:10–12, ESV)

In his parables Jesus warns his followers about the testing and temptation that will come: those who lack deep roots will dry up and wither away in the temptation. He commends the disciples for being with him through trials, "You are those who have stood by me in my trials" (Luke 22:28, NRSVCE), but then, soon after, cautions them about the need to stay awake and not succumb to temptation: "Why are you sleeping? Rise and pray that you may not enter into temptation" (Luke 22:46, ESV). They fail in this test, but Jesus restores them when he appears to them after his Resurrection.

The apostolic letters of the New Testament underline this call to endure trials and suffering as disciples of the Lord. Recounting his own persecutions and suffering, Paul couldn't be clearer about the expectation we all should have: All who desire to live a godly Christian life will experience persecution (2 Tim 3:12). In a passage that has always brought great comfort to me, Paul assures us that the grace of God will see us through the trials we face: "No testing has overtaken you that is not common to everyone. God is faithful, and he will not let you be tested beyond your strength, but with the testing he will also provide the way out so that you may be able to endure it" (1 Cor 10:13, NRSVCE).

We are given more than just a promise that God will help us get through our trials. We are assured that God is also present *in the midst* of our sufferings, giving us both comfort and joy on the way. In his Second Letter to the Corinthians, Paul recounts in vivid language the desperate and fearful sufferings that he has recently passed through. He was oppressed, beaten down, and even crushed, despairing of life—but God rescued him and brought him through the trial (2 Cor 1:8–9). Further on, Paul speaks about being afflicted, perplexed, persecuted, and struck down (2 Cor 4:8–9).

This is not light stuff—Paul was clearly pressed to the edge of his endurance and even beyond. But at the same time he gives witness to the consolation or encouragement that he was granted in the midst of these sufferings: "For just as the sufferings of Christ abound in us, so too through Christ does our comfort abound" (2 Cor 1:5).

One of the most jarring things in the New Testament is how frequently suffering and joy are combined and joined. This is *not* the way we normally experience life: if we are suffering, we are not joyful; if we are joyful, we are not suffering. But through the example of Christ and the power of the indwelling Spirit, we are made capable of rejoicing in the midst of our trials. We already saw how Jesus calls his disciples to "rejoice" when they are persecuted. This joy in the midst of trial and suffering reappears several times. James tells us to count it all as joy when we encounter various trials, because we know that such testing produces greater faithfulness in us (Jas 1:2–3). In the same vein, Peter exhorts us not to be surprised at the "fiery ordeals" that come upon us as though they were something strange. Rather, we ought to expect these trials and rejoice in them because they give us the opportunity to share in Christ's own sufferings (1 Pet 4:12–14). And because we have received the Holy Spirit in our hearts, we can, with Paul, "rejoice" in our sufferings, knowing that as we endure them in faith we will grow to become more like Christ himself.

If this were not enough, we are also comforted in the midst of our sufferings by the sure knowledge that, as we faithfully endure, we can look forward with joy to our eternal inheritance in the next life. The Letter to the Hebrews tells us that Jesus himself found joy in this expectation: ". . . who for the joy that was set before him endured the cross, despising the shame, and is seated at the right hand of the throne of God" (Heb 12:2, ESV). Paul confesses the same: "I consider that the sufferings of this present time are not worth comparing with the glory about to be revealed to us" (Rom 8:18, NRSVCE). In another place Paul speaks about the general dissolution of our bodies as we age, saying that though our physical bodies are wasting away, our inner spiritual nature is being renewed in Christ every day. The temporary bodily affliction that we experience now is preparing for us an "eternal weight of glory" beyond anything we can imagine (2 Cor 4:16–17).

READINESS TO SUFFER WITH JOY

Commenting on the *flight from suffering* in our current culture, Patricia Snow wonders whether people today will be able to receive and pass along to others the call to endure the cross and the suffering that Christian discipleship entails:

> In a world of recovering codependents, God's word is still reverberating, but man is too timorous to repeat it. He is too fragile and insecure, too existentially touchy and emotionally raw. Suspicious of others' influence and terrified of exercising his own, frightened of suffering himself but

even more unnerved by the thought of others suffering—how can such a person receive Christ or
offer him to others, when either to receive or propose Christ is always, at the same time, to receive
and propose his cross? In a suffering-averse world,
handing on the Gospel is almost impossible.[11]

Almost impossible, but not quite. Our love of creature
comforts and our flight from personal hardship make it
extremely difficult to embrace the call to bear the cross
and suffer with Christ.

One conclusion that I draw: if we are to reinvigorate
Christian discipleship, then we also need to re-equip ourselves to embrace adventurously the trials and suffering
that come in the wake of following Christ. How to accomplish this? The great adventures that we love to read
and watch have the potential to open our eyes and to inspire us to be (and to become) the kind of people who can
endure hardship and who are ready to suffer for what is
good and right, whether this comes through the example
of Puddleglum, Frodo Baggins, or others. Even more, a
good dose of the heroic lives of the saints strengthens the
heart and invigorates the soul. But what we need most of
all is what enabled these very saints to endure trials and
suffering for the sake of Christ joyfully. We need *the Holy
Spirit in person*, active in our lives, giving help for every
occasion, and encouraging us to press on in hope through
the trials that beset us because of "the joy set before us."

---

[11] Patricia Snow, "Empathy is not Charity," *First Things* (October 2017),
https://www.firstthings.com/article/2017/10/empathy-is-not-charity.

* *Portrait* *
ST. JOHN OF THE CROSS

St. John of the Cross had every reason to complain and become embittered by the many hardships that was his lot to endure. When a young boy, he lost his father; along with his mother and sisters he grew up in continual poverty and want. Moving from an orphanage school to a Jesuit college, he finally joined the Carmelites and was ordained a priest at age twenty-five. Shortly afterwards he met St. Teresa of Avila and joined the reform movement within the Carmelite order. As opposition to the reform from within the Carmelites mounted, John was at one point taken captive, flogged, and accused of insubordination. When he refused to renounce the reform because of a vow he had taken, he was imprisoned. For nine months he was held in solitary confinement, much of it in a six-by-ten-foot closet, suffering extremes of heat and cold, ravaged by disease and growing frail. One night, guided by a vision, he escaped and found refuge within a convent of Carmelite women of the reform movement. Though sick and emaciated from his confinement, he witnessed to the sisters the love of God and the blessing of suffering for his sake:

> It is an astonishing scene: a scarecrow of a man, at death's door, famished, filthy, beaten to a pulp and starved of human companionship, does not ask for food or drink or a safe haven. Instead he only wants to speak of the goodness and beauty of God; his keenest desire is to share his love for the One who came to him in the darkness, who

revealed himself most clearly and alluringly in the midst of crucifixion.[12]

John of the Cross not only wrote powerfully about the love of God in the midst of suffering and darkness, he experienced this profoundly in his own life. He continues to model for us how someone can embrace trials and suffering with joy in the costly adventure of Christian discipleship.

[12] Jerome K. Williams, *True Reformers* (Greenwood Village, CO: Augustine Institute, 2017), 203.

·✺·

CHAPTER SEVEN

TRUE FRIENDSHIP IN THE ADVENTURE OF DISCIPLESHIP

For without friends no one would choose to live, though he had all other goods.

—Aristotle[1]

The most universal and, in our opinion, the noblest of all forms of interhuman communication, the only one capable of dissolving our loneliness, is friendship.

—Ignace Lepp[2]

Whether it develops between persons of the same or opposite sex, friendship represents a great good for all. It leads to spiritual communion.

CCC 2347

---

[1] Aristotle, *The Nichomachean Ethics*, VIII.1, trans. W. D. Ross (Oxford: Oxford University Press, 1998), 192.

[2] Ignace Lepp, *The Ways of Friendship*, trans. Bernard Murchland (New York: MacMillan, 1966), 21.

WE live in a world deeply hungry, even desperate, for friendship. But it seems that true friendship remains in short supply. We now have multiple social networking sites where people can claim "friends" by the hundreds, but these same people report being lonelier than ever. It is not difficult to see why. Social networking can be a fine way to keep in touch with friends or to pass along information, but it simply does not serve well as a vehicle for making real friends or deepening true friendship. Christine Rosen explains why she thinks this is so:

> But "friendship" in these virtual spaces is thoroughly different from real-world friendship. In its traditional sense, friendship is a relationship which, broadly speaking, involves the sharing of mutual interests, reciprocity, trust, and the revelation of intimate details over time and within specific social (and cultural) contexts. Because friendship depends on mutual revelations that are concealed from the rest of the world, it can only flourish within the boundaries of privacy; the idea of public friendship is an oxymoron.[3]

As we shall see, having groups of friends or even communities of friends is entirely possible, but this involves more than gathering up hundreds of friends online. If we take short-cuts on the road to friendship we will fail to gain the real thing and its counterfeits will only leave us more

---

[3] Christine Rosen, "Virtual Friendship and the New Narcissism," *The New Atlantis* (Summer 2007): 26.

desperately lonely and vulnerable than before.

Our hunger for authentic friendship is not a sign of weakness or immaturity; it is part of being human. If the wisdom of the wise can be trusted, friendship is one of the greatest "goods" that humans can experience. Aristotle (fourth century BC) concludes that "the man who is to be happy will therefore need virtuous friends."[4] Aelred of Rievaulx (twelfth century) states that "scarcely any happiness whatever can exist among mankind without friendship."[5] A contemporary Catholic psychiatrist, Ignace Lepp, reckons that "friendship represents one of the most precious values of the human condition. It is certainly worth the effort to commit ourselves courageously to the experience of friendship."[6]

This chapter is about the central place of *friendship* in the costly adventure of discipleship. If friendship is centrally important—and I believe that it is—then this shows that Christian discipleship requires and thrives in a *communal* context. We are not lone Christians walking a solitary pilgrimage of faith. Rather, we are banded together with other companions in a common pilgrimage, serving together, fighting together against a common foe, and helping each other along the way. Crucially, this friendship is not merely instrumental; it is not something that simply helps us make progress on the path, like a bicycle or a golf cart. The *goal* and *end* of eternal life is communion (*koinonia*) with God and with one another. Our friendships here

---

[4] Aristotle, *The Nichomachean Ethics*, IX.9, 241.

[5] Aelred of Rievaulx, *Spiritual Friendship*, 2.10, trans. Mary Eugenia Laker (Kalamazoo: Cistercian Publications, 1977), 71.

[6] Lepp, *The Ways of Friendship*, 127.

in this life are the training-ground and foretaste of the friendship that will be ours eternally. Christian discipleship at its core is also a school of friendship.

This chapter and the next really are about the two great commandments, "love of neighbor" and "love of God," respectively. To investigate all that is contained in these two great commandments is far beyond what I can attempt. Instead, I will pursue the more limited goal of sketching the place of *friendship* in the life of the Christian disciple. This chapter deals with our companionship and friendship with others; the next and final chapter concerns our friendship and communion with God.

To begin, we will try to gain a basic understanding of what friendship is. Drawing on the wisdom of many writers, both ancient and contemporary, I hope to offer a sketch of what friendship looks like. Then following our pattern, I will illustrate what friendship is by looking at models of companionship in the adventures and stories that we love. The first example returns us to J. R. R. Tolkien and *The Lord of the Rings*: I can think of no better account of how friendships are forged than what we find among the members of the Fellowship of the Ring. The second example turns to the most popular of Jane Austen's novels to see how two pairs of friends help (or hinder) one another through the ups and downs of courtship and marriage. To conclude, I will turn to a real-life example and shine the spotlight on the celebrated spiritual friendship between St. Francis de Sales and St. Jane de Chantal. This will help us grasp the specific qualities of friendship in Christ.

WHAT FRIENDSHIP IS

Defining friendship is a notoriously difficult thing to do. In the opening comments of his justly renowned treatise on friendship, Aristotle admits that "not a few things about friendship are matters of debate."[7] Most of us can identify who our friends are and can recount the few people that constitute our closest friends at any given stage of life, but it's not easy to describe just why we count them as friends and even harder to put into words what friendship is. When we define friendship too narrowly or in lofty and exalted terms, we end up excluding most people from ever having experienced friendship! And this is not helpful.

My goal is to offer a general sketch of what friendship is by describing five qualities that tend to mark the experience of real friendship, in the conviction that all of us, according to our own capability, are called to embrace the great good that friendship brings.

1. *True friendship includes genuine concern for the good of our friends.* By all accounts, an essential quality of true friendship is that we seek the good and well-being of our friend. I may greatly benefit from my friends in many ways (and I certainly do), but the mark of friendship is that I am seeking not my own good, but that of my friend. In his discussion of friendship, Thomas Aquinas gives special emphasis to this quality: "It pertains to the essential meaning of friendship for the lover to will the fulfillment of the desire of the beloved, because he wishes the good

---

[7] Aristotle, *The Nichomachean Ethics*, VIII.1, 193.

and the perfect for the beloved."[8] Many of us may have friends because they are *useful* to us or because they give us *pleasure*. But this is an imperfect kind of friendship: we are making use of "friends" really in order to love ourselves. Genuine friendship demands that we break away from the gravitational pull of self-love and seek the good of another for his or her own sake. True friends are concerned for the good of each other.

2. *True friendship involves common interests and sharing.* Friends normally share common interests: sports, music, dancing, books, concerts, ideas, or common causes. A common interest is prominent in some friendships, but may play a less significant role in others. Often it is around these common activities that personal communion between friends develops. Aristotle describes it this way: "For friendship is a partnership, and as a man is to himself, so is he to his friend."[9] Ignace Lepp says that "all friendship implies a certain degree of communion; a certain likeness must exist between friends, a more or less essential community of interests."[10] Aquinas, too, uses the language of likeness and unity to describe how love between friends develops.[11]

What does this mean? When people become friends

[8] Thomas Aquinas, *Summa contra Gentiles*, III.95.5, trans. Joseph Kenny (New York: Hanover House, 1955–1957), http://dhspriory.org/thomas/ContraGentiles.htm.

[9] Aristotle, *Nichomachean Ethics*, IX.12, 246.

[10] Lepp, *The Ways of Friendship*, 127.

[11] See St. Thomas Aquinas, *Commentary on the Gospel of John: Chapters 13–21* (§ 2036), trans. Fabian Larcher and James A. Weisheipl (Washington, DC: Catholic University of America Press, 2010), 117.

they typically experience a common interest that draws them together and gives them joy in one another. They become like each other in certain ways and experience the love of friendship for each other because of that likeness and unity. This doesn't mean that we become clones of one another or all begin to look and act the same. Far from it. Friendship flourishes when each of us, in our distinctive personalities, are joined together in a joyful bond with others because we are able to share good things together.

3. *True friendship brings about a certain equality between friends.* In healthy friendship there is no desire to dominate or "crush" the other. Instead, friendship brings about a kind of equality among the friends, such that each has equal standing in the relationship. When friendship arises between people who are *unequal* in age, wisdom, influence, experience, or talent, their friendship tends to minimize those differences over time and bring them together in a common unity. The friendship that develops, for example, between Gandalf and Pippin in *The Lord of the Rings* illustrates this quality of friendship. The great wizard and the youthful hobbit have little in common and are hugely unequal in stature, ability, and experience. But thrown together in a common quest, they develop a delightful, affectionate friendship where each can "needle" the other because of genuine knowledge of the other. Pointing to the kind of love that binds friends together, Aristotle observes that "it is in this way more than any other that even unequals can be friends; they can be equalized."[12]

---

[12] Aristotle, *Nichomachean Ethics*, VIII.8, 206.

4. *True friendship is personal but not exclusive or jealous.*
True and mature friendship is personal but it is not jealous in the way that romantic or erotic love is. This is one of the clearest differences between friendship and sexual love. C. S. Lewis speaks to this quality of friendship: "Hence true Friendship is the least jealous of loves. Two friends delight to be joined by a third, and three by a fourth, if only the newcomer is qualified to become a real friend."[13] While we typically imagine friendship between two people only, friendship can be shared with others and good friends are glad to be among three or more. I may enjoy spending time alone with my good friend, but I wouldn't become possessive or jealous if he or she was spending time with other friends. According to Ignace Lepp, these other friendships can in fact strengthen and invigorate the friendship that I have with that person: "There is no place for jealousy in a friendship worthy of the name. . . . The friendship of a friend for other persons in no way affects the friendship that exists between him and me. On the contrary, we can only benefit from the enrichment which he acquires through other friendships."[14] This personal but non-exclusive quality of friendship makes it an extremely blessed gift for the adventure of costly discipleship. I can be strengthened by many friendships, each having its own particular quality, but I can also rejoice in the many friendships that my friends have with each other—and together we can be a band of friends on pilgrimage.

13 C. S. Lewis, *The Four Loves* (New York: Harcourt Brace, 1960), 92.
14 Lepp, *The Ways of Friendship*, 54.

5. *True friendship builds on and increases goodness.* As parents know well, it makes a great deal of difference how children pick their friends. If we befriend wild, vicious, and unjust people, we will tend to become like them. If we befriend good, generous, and just people, we are likely to grow in these virtues. There is a kind of friendship among thieves, but true friendship can only flourish among those who are aiming at the good. Aristotle laid it down that "perfect friendship is the friendship of men who are good, and alike in virtue."[15] St. Francis de Sales offers this advice when it comes to choosing our friends: "Love one another with a great charitable love, but only have a friendship with those who can communicate virtuous things with you, and the more exquisite the virtues that you will put in your relationship the more perfect will your friendship be."[16] Thus, friendship can be a vehicle for mutual growth in virtue. Because friends are seeking together what is good, they can be open and honest and see each other more as they really are. "We accept our friends without illusion, with full knowledge of their virtues and faults."[17] As I seek goodness and holiness, I fit myself for richer and more profound friendships. I become the kind of person that I myself would seek for a friend.

At this point let me pose a question: is there anything distinctive about Christian friendship, about the quality of friendship between disciples of our Lord? In Christ,

---

[15] Aristotle, *Nichomachean Ethics*, VIII.3, 196.

[16] St. Francis de Sales, *Introduction to the Devout Life*, III.19, trans. André Ravier, *Francis de Sales: Sage and Saint* (San Francisco: Ignatius Press, 1988), 138.

[17] Lepp, *The Ways of Friendship*, 51–52.

friendships become re-centered and newly powered. They have all the human qualities of normal friendships, but Christ is invited into the center of the friendship and the Spirit can empower that friendship from within. Francis de Sales speaks eloquently about the special excellence that friendship in Christ possesses: "It will be excellent because it comes from God, excellent because it tends toward God, excellent because its good is God, excellent because it will endure eternally in God."[18] This makes Christian friendship especially joyful and hopeful. In the midst of sadness and loss, we maintain full confidence that we will live with our friends eternally. Aelred of Rievaulx captures the joy of this enduring friendship: "This is true and eternal friendship, which begins in this life and is perfected in the next, which here belongs to the few where few are good, but there belongs to all where all are good."[19]

So, what is friendship? Friendship is a great gift that is meant to characterize our common pilgrimage. True friends aim for each other's good. They join in common interests and grow together in unity and likeness. They love one another but are glad to see their friendships extend to others. They pursue a common good and help one another grow in a life of virtue and holiness. With this sketch of friendship in hand, we will now turn to two examples of natural friendship and one of spiritual friendship in Christ.

[18] *Introduction to the Devout Life*, III, 19; Ravier, *Francis de Sales*, 138.
[19] Aelred, *Spiritual Friendship*, 3.80, 111.

THE FORGING OF FRIENDSHIPS IN THE FELLOWSHIP OF THE RING

With remarkable artistry, J. R. R. Tolkien weaves a tale that displays many varied and impressive friendships. Readers are typically so caught up with the plot of *The Lord of the Rings* that they hardly notice the deep friendships that form between the four hobbits (Frodo, Sam, Merry, and Pippin), the wizard Gandalf, the dwarf Gimli, the Elf Legolas, and the man Aragorn.

The conspiratorial friendship of the hobbits for Frodo is revealed when Frodo is planning to announce his departure and slip away from them into danger by himself. The other three are having none of it: they know what he is planning and are determined to go with him into danger. Merry tells Frodo, "After all, you must remember that we know you well, and are often with you. We can usually guess what you are thinking. . . . You are not going to escape so easily!"[20] Frodo is unhappy with this response and tries to convince them the he must go away alone. Hearing the details of their conspiracy, Frodo accuses them of being untrustworthy. Merry again responds, showing the bond of friendship they have: "You can trust us to stick to you through thick and thin—to the bitter end. . . . But you cannot trust us to let you face trouble alone, and go off without a word. We are your friends, Frodo."[21] Frodo, overwhelmed with their loyalty and willing sacrifice, relents and gladly welcomes them as companions. These deep bonds of friendship will be tested many times over

[20] Tolkien, *The Fellowship of the Ring*, 136–37.
[21] Tolkien, *The Fellowship of the Ring*, 138.

in the story that follows, but the hobbits remain true to the end. Their loyal comradery will prove crucial for the fulfillment of the quest.

Tolkien revisits this deep friendship between the four hobbits in the final pages of the story. Frodo is leaving Middle-earth, setting sail with Bilbo, Gandalf, and others to the eternal lands. Sam accompanies him to the havens, but at the last moment, Merry and Pippin come galloping up to say their farewells. This time it is Pippin who speaks: "You tried to give us the slip once before and failed, Frodo.... This time you have nearly succeeded, but you have failed again. It was not Sam, though, who gave you away this time, but Gandalf himself." Gandalf then speaks about the final ending of the Fellowship: "Well, here at last, dear friends, on the shores of the Sea comes the end of our fellowship in Middle-earth. Go in peace! I will not say: do not weep; for not all tears are evil."[22]

Another remarkable friendship is that between Legolas and Gimli. In Middle-earth, Elves and dwarves are known for being cold and even hostile toward one another, yet these two form an unusual companionship that amazes all around them. They display friendly competition over how many Orcs each was able to kill, but the deep bond of affection between them shines out even in the competition. In this friendship we see the real possibility of two individuals from the most estranged backgrounds able to form a profound and attractive friendship. After the quest is achieved, when the fellowship is about to break up, Legolas and Gimli go off together—just the

[22] Tolkien, *The Return of the King*, 346–47.

two of them—to show each other the wonders they have found: Legolas wishes to show Gimli the enchanted forest of Fangorn and Gimli wants to show Legolas the wonders of the glittering caves of Aglarond. This is just what great friends do: they share with each other the joy of the great things they have discovered. It is no accident that in the appendices to *The Lord of the Rings*, Tolkien records that, after all the others from the Fellowship had died or travelled to the undying lands, Legolas set sail with Gimli the dwarf to travel to the undying lands across the sea.[23] Their friendship endures to the end.

One of the most charming scenes in the book occurs when Gimli, Legolas, and Aragorn arrive at Isengard only to find Merry and Pippen eating, drinking, and smoking pipes at the gate. Gimli is nearly overcome with conflicting emotions of exasperation and joy. His fierce language only underlines the deep affection that has been formed between him, Legolas, and the two hobbits:

> And what about your companions? What about Legolas and me? . . . You rascals, you woolly-footed and wool-pated truants! A fine hunt you have led us! Two hundred leagues, through fen and forest, battle and death, to rescue you. And here we find you feasting and idling—and smoking! Smoking! Where did you come by the weed, you villains? Hammer and tongs! I am so torn between rage and joy, that if I do not burst, it will be a marvel![24]

---

[23] Tolkien, *The Return of the King*, 433.
[24] Tolkien, *The Two Towers*, 191.

Recognizing the playfulness in these strong words, the riders of Rohan break into laughter, while King Theoden says: "It cannot be doubted that we witness the meeting of dear friends."[25] Tolkien offers here a penetrating depiction of the forging of masculine friendship in the midst of a common mission.

Readers (and viewers) of *The Lord of the Rings* are rightly captured by the glorious quest and the working out of a great plot. But this tale is equally about the forging of true friendships. It displays what true companions can be: Frodo and Sam, Gandalf and Pippen, Bilbo and Frodo, Legolas and Gimli, even Treebeard and the hobbits. Why is it that so many of us go back to this story again and again? We return in part, I believe, because we are entranced and captivated by the excellence of the friendships that we find there.

FRIENDSHIP IN *PRIDE AND PREJUDICE*

The novels of Jane Austen, and the TV-film versions of them, have proved enormously popular in the past generation, giving rise to fan clubs, festivals, and all varieties of spin-off literature. Of her six complete novels, the most popular and iconic is *Pride and Prejudice*, a story about courtship and marriage, but also and more profoundly about human character and growth in virtue. The two central figures, Elizabeth Bennet and Fitzwilliam Darcy, are magnetic and intriguing characters whose relations are initially marked by pride (especially on his side) and prejudice (especially on her side); by novel's end they end up

[25] Tolkien, *The Two Towers*, 191.

in love with each other and married. The narrative of this unlikely courtship, aided by a cast of interesting and entertaining characters, makes *Pride and Prejudice* a perennial favorite. I wish to explore here, not the relationship between Elizabeth and Darcy (as fascinating as this is), but the quality of friendship between two pairs of friends: on the one side, between Elizabeth and her older sister Jane, and on the other, between Mr. Darcy and his closest friend, Mr. Charles Bingley.

Jane Austen makes clear from the start of the novel that, of the five Bennet girls, Jane and Elizabeth are the only two who have any sense. Austen herself describes the youngest three in terms that show their lack of good sense, and their father describes them several times as three of the silliest girls in England. In contrast, Jane and Elizabeth are marked out by all observers as intelligent, sensible, and worthy of admiration. They are likely candidates to form a friendship based on a shared goodness. Nevertheless, Austen casts them as opposites in character and disposition. Jane is supremely "good," always thinking the best of people and never saying a bad word about anyone. Elizabeth respects this deep goodness in Jane, but also chides her for failing to see people as they really are: "Oh! you are a great deal too apt, you know, to like people in general. You never see a fault in anybody. All the world are good and agreeable in your eyes. I never heard you speak ill of a human being in your life."[26] Elizabeth is in character the opposite of Jane: witty, insightful, sharp-tongued, and quick to spot the faults and follies of others. One of

[26] Jane Austen, *Pride and Prejudice* (New York: E. P. Dutton, 1976), 16.

the charms of the book is the sympathetic friendship that develops between these two sisters of very different gifts and dispositions.

A notable mark of their friendship is how fully they identify with the concerns and well-being of the other: both are quick to set aside their own problems to share in those of the other, and both genuinely rejoice in the good fortune of the other. When Jane is being singled out for attention by the amiable and wealthy Mr. Bingley, Elizabeth is stirred not to jealousy but to delight for her: "Elizabeth felt Jane's pleasure."[27] Later, when the dread news of their sister Lydia's elopement reaches Elizabeth in far-off Derbyshire, she is distraught with what this will mean for her own fortunes, but even more so she wishes to share with Jane the burdens that have fallen upon her: "She was wild to be at home—to hear, to see, to be upon the spot to share with Jane in the cares that must now fall wholly upon her, in a family so deranged, a father absent, a mother incapable of exertion, and requiring constant attendance."[28] Upon arrival she expresses her concern for what her sister has borne: "Oh that I had been with you! You have had every care and anxiety upon yourself alone."[29]

Again, when Jane becomes engaged to Mr. Bingley, Elizabeth's expression of joy for her sister couldn't be greater: "Elizabeth's congratulations were given with a sincerity, a warmth, a delight, which words could but poorly express. Every sentence of kindness was a fresh

[27] Austen, *Pride and Prejudice*, 14.
[28] Austen, *Pride and Prejudice*, 295.
[29] Austen, *Pride and Prejudice*, 308.

source of happiness to Jane."[30] Jane reciprocates these congratulations once she overcomes her amazement that Elizabeth and Mr. Darcy are actually engaged to be married: "Now I am quite happy . . . for you will be as happy as myself."[31] The two friends seem to experience greater joy for the other than for themselves.

Jane and Elizabeth are shown talking together, usually late at night, on many occasions in the novel. Normally it is Elizabeth who provides Jane with insight and encouragement, though clearly both benefit from these intimate exchanges and look to the other for wisdom and perspective. Shortly after her dramatic refusal of Mr. Darcy's advances, Elizabeth finds comfort in sharing this secret with Jane: "The tumult of Elizabeth's mind was allayed by this conversation [with Jane]. She had got rid of two of the secrets which had weighed on her for a fortnight, and was certain of a willing listener in Jane, whenever she might wish to talk again of either."[32] Yet the two sisters did not share everything with the other; both held back when concerned with over-burdening or wounding the other. Jane hid her deep grief following Mr. Bingley's departure, while Elizabeth kept secret the full report of Mr. Darcy's activities. Yet in the end, all is revealed and they are able to fully sympathize and rejoice with each other.

Notably, the deep friendship of these two sisters was not threatened by the prospect of marriage and the arrival of a lover for each of them. Certainly their intimacy would

---

[30] Austen, *Pride and Prejudice*, 364.
[31] Austen, *Pride and Prejudice*, 396.
[32] Austen, *Pride and Prejudice*, 239–40.

no longer remain as it was, but the sturdiness of their deep regard for each other only helped them to seek the good of the other. In a manner pleasurable both to the two sisters and to the reader, Austen arranges at book's end for the two happy couples to settle close to one another: Mr. Bingley "bought an estate in a neighbouring county to Derbyshire, and Jane and Elizabeth, in addition to every other source of happiness, were within thirty miles of each other."[33] This deep and admirable friendship, we are assured, will continue throughout their lives.

The friendship between Mr. Darcy and Mr. Bingley receives less direct attention in the novel, but through descriptions by the author and fragments of conversations, we can gain some sense of the quality of their relationship and its development. At one point, Colonel Fitzwilliam acknowledges that Bingley is "a great friend of Darcy's."[34] But it is Jane Austen herself as narrator who introduces the relationship and describes its character: "Between [Bingley] and Darcy there was a very steady friendship, in spite of great opposition of character." Darcy was drawn to Bingley "by the easiness, openness, and ductility of his temper, though no disposition could offer a greater contrast to his own." For his part, Bingley relied on Darcy's regard and had the highest opinion of Darcy's judgments. Austen informs us as to why: "In understanding, Darcy was the superior. Bingley was by no means deficient, but Darcy was clever." Yet Darcy had his faults: "He was at the same time haughty, reserved, and fastidious, and his man-

[33] Austen, *Pride and Prejudice*, 407.
[34] Austen, *Pride and Prejudice*, 195.

ners, though well-bred, were not inviting. In that respect his friend had greatly the advantage." The result was that "Bingley was sure of being liked wherever he appeared, Darcy was continually giving offense."[35] This is a friendship of opposites: each one supplied something of what the other lacked.

We are given the impression that Darcy and Bingley expressed their friendship largely through the activities they pursued together: riding, shooting, and spending time in the company of close-knit friends. From what we can glean, their friendship was anchored more in common activities than intimate conversation. Darcy tended to dominate the relationship as the stronger of the two, but at points Bingley shows his spirit. In one interchange, Darcy charges Bingley with indirectly boasting of his defects and failures. Bingley responds with a swipe at Darcy's cold and forbidding temper: "I assure you, that if Darcy were not such a great tall fellow, in comparison with myself, I should not pay him half so much deference. I declare I do not know a more awful object than Darcy, on particular occasions, and in particular places; at his own house especially."[36] The two friends are plainly aware of each other's faults and failings, but as is typical among men, they find it difficult to speak of these faults to each other easily or without tension.

In the central part of the story, Bingley withdraws from the narrative, only to return towards the close of the novel. Darcy had played the crucial role in persuading

---

[35] Austen, *Pride and Prejudice*, 18.
[36] Austen, *Pride and Prejudice*, 53.

Bingley to withdraw from the relationship with Jane Bennet. In simple terms, he was the cause of their break-up, and felt justified in so acting because of the undesirable connections that this marriage would incur. In hindsight, Darcy realizes that he was wrong to interfere, and in a conversation with Elizabeth Bennet, he recounts his direct apology to Bingley: "On the evening before my going to London . . . I made a confession to him, which I believe I ought to have made long ago. I told him of all that had occurred to make my former interference in his affairs absurd and impertinent." The result: "[Bingley] was angry. But his anger, I am persuaded, lasted no longer than he remained in any doubt of your sister's sentiments. He has heartily forgiven me now."[37] This is most impressive (and rare). Darcy has the courage and humility to admit his fault and he offers a plain and unequivocal apology to his friend. And Bingley, though bruised, rebounds and forgives his friend *heartily*. As the story closes, we find the two of them together once again, happily married to the two Bennet sisters and living in close proximity to one another.

Pride and Prejudice, besides being a captivating story full of fascinating characters, offers a window onto human virtue and vice, nobility and silliness, admirable characters and despicable rogues. It also presents a delightful account of two friendships that not only withstand severe tests but grow—by means of these tests—in goodness and faithfulness.

---

[37] Austen, *Pride and Prejudice*, 393–94.

SPIRITUAL FRIENDSHIP

When we come to examine the relationship between Francis de Sales (1567–1622) and Jane de Chantal (1572–1641), we are looking in on what one author calls "the birth, development, and flowering of one of the greatest friendships that ever bound a director and his disciple."[38] When they first met during a Lenten retreat given by Francis in 1604, he was the bishop of Geneva and she was the recently widowed mother of four children. Wendy Wright sums up their relationship over the following eighteen years:

> Between the years 1604 and 1622 Francis de Sales and Jane de Chantal shared in a spiritual friendship of intense and mutual creativity. Their relationship began in the context of spiritual direction when Jane, a young widow, sought out the charismatic bishop from Savoy who was gaining a reputation as a preacher and guide of souls. By the time he died eighteen years later, they had co-founded the Visitation of Holy Mary, a community for women unique in the history of religious life ... and cultivated a unique friendship that brought them both to the fullness of their human potential and closer to the dearest longing of their hearts—the radical and self-giving love of God.[39]

---

[38] Ravier, *Francis de Sales*, 137.
[39] Wendy Wright, "'Hearts Have a Secret Language': The Spiritual Friendship of Francis de Sales and Jane de Chantal," *Vincentian Heritage Journal* 11 (1990): 45–46.

Over these years, Francis and Jane frequently wrote letters to each other. Scholars estimate that Francis sent approximately 400 letters, while Jane wrote somewhat fewer but still very many in return. We have half of the letters that Francis wrote to Jane, but because Jane burned her letters after Francis's death, we do not possess her part of the correspondence. Based on the evidence of the letters, Henri Nouwen calls their relationship a "Jesus-centered, affectionate friendship," and he points to the common love of God that anchored their friendship from first to last:

> What is most obvious from this correspondence is that Jesus stands in the center of the lives of Francis and Jane. The love of God revealed in Jesus Christ pervades every line of the letters they both wrote. They are two people whose friendship is solidly anchored in their common love of God. It is a mediated friendship. There lies the secret of their freedom and their fruitfulness.[40]

Many people questioned then—and still question today—whether true friendship is really possible between a man and a woman who are not married to each other. Francis himself cautions against the spiritual dangers that may arise in a friendship between members of the opposite sex:

---

[40] Henri Nouwen, "Preface," Francis de Sales and Jane de Chantal, *Letters of Spiritual Direction*, trans. Péronne Marie Thibert, eds. Wendy M. Wright and Joseph F. Power (New York: Paulist, 1988), 3.

We must be on our guard not to be deceived in making friendships, especially between persons of the opposite sexes, for not unfrequently Satan deludes those who love one another. They may begin with a virtuous affection, but if discretion be lacking, frivolity will creep in, and then sensuality, till their love becomes carnal: even in spiritual love there is a danger if people are not on the watch, although it is not so easy to be deluded therein.[41]

By all accounts Francis and Jane succeeded in finding a genuine friendship that remained grounded in Christ and avoided romantic entanglement. In a letter to Jane in the first year of their acquaintance, Francis acknowledges: "I must tell you that I have never understood that there was any bond between us carrying with it any obligation but that of charity and true Christian friendship, what St. Paul calls 'the bond of perfection' (Col 3:14)."[42] In his letters, Francis consistently urges Jane to completely abandon herself to the love of God:

I shall never stop praying God to perfect His work in you, that is, to further your excellent desire and plan to attain the fullness of Christian life, a desire which you should cherish and nurture tenderly in your heart; consider it a work of the Holy Spirit and a spark of His divine flame.[43]

---

[41] Francis, *Introduction to the Devout Life*, III.20 (New York: Vintage Books, 2002), 133.

[42] Francis de Sales and Jane de Chantal, *Letters of Spiritual Direction*, 127.

[43] Francis de Sales and Jane de Chantal, *Letters of Spiritual Direction*, 123.

And while Francis was the primary care-giver in providing spiritual direction for Jane, he also took seriously Jane's concern for his spiritual and physical well-being and acted upon her entreaties:

> But do you know what I am going to promise you? To take better care of my health from now on—even though I have always taken better care of myself than I actually deserve; and thanks be to God, I am feeling quite well now, since I've totally cut out staying up late and the excessive writing that I used to do at that hour. And I've been eating more sensibly too.[44]

According to Wendy Wright, there was a genuine reciprocity in their friendship, each receiving something from the other that made them more effective servants of God: "He provided ballast for her deep waters; she provided depth and passion for him. This was true not simply on the personal level of friendship but in prayer as well."[45]

Francis sums up the difference between worldly and spiritual friendship in this way: "Worldly friendship is profuse in honeyed words, passionate endearments, commendations of beauty and sensual charms, while true friendship speaks a simple honest language, lauding nought save the Grace of God, its one only foundation."[46] These two saints seemed to have a particular capacity for

---

[44] Francis de Sales and Jane de Chantal, *Letters of Spiritual Direction*, 144.

[45] Wright, "Hearts Have a Secret Language," 53.

[46] Francis, *Introduction to the Devout Life*, III.20, 133.

deep friendship and found in each other someone who possessed the same single-minded love for God. For most of us, this quality of friendship in Christ may seem unattainable. Yet it remains a great example of how God our Father, the author of our great and costly adventure, provides friends along the way for his followers for mutual help and joy on our common pilgrimage. The bond of friendship remains one of God's richest blessings to his disciples.

FRIENDSHIP IN THE ADVENTURE OF COSTLY DISCIPLESHIP

C. S. Lewis reminds us that friends, especially friends who share a commitment to a common Christian discipleship, are a great gift from God. Friendship, like any other created good thing, can become something that we idolize; friends can take the place of God and we can relate to friendship as if it can save us and give us life. But only God can give life.

> Friendship is not a reward for our discrimination and good taste in finding one another out. It is the instrument by which God reveals to each the beauties of all the others. . . . At this feast it is He who has spread the board and it is He who has chosen the guests. It is He, we may dare to hope, who sometimes does, and always should, preside. Let us not reckon without our Host.[47]

---

[47] Lewis, *The Four Loves*, 126.

Who are the people that we are called to befriend? Who are the people God has placed in our lives to be friends for us—friends for the journey, a gift from his hand? And how can we nourish this friendship and recognize the great gift that it is for us? We can be inspired and informed by the great friendships that we read about or witness personally, but we need to live with and befriend the *real* people that God has placed in our lives. I am encouraged and en-visioned by witnessing the deep friendships between the members of the Fellowship of the Ring, and by seeing the Christ-centered friendship between Francis and Jane. But I cannot have them as my friends—not yet at any rate! The task for each of us is to cherish and receive with gratitude the friends for the journey that God has given to us, and to increase our own capacity for friendship, so that we might not squander the gift of God or fail to be a true friend to our fellow-travelers.

For this task, the words of Christ himself provide the anchor we need. He has declared us—his disciples—to be his friends. "I no longer call you servants—for the servant does not know what his master is doing—but I have called you friends" (John 15:15). And if we are his friends, then we are friends of one another, called to lay down our lives daily for the love of each other: "No one has greater love than this, to lay down one's life for one's friends" (John 15:13, NRSVCE).

* *Portrait* *
DAVID AND JONATHAN

The relationship between Jonathan and David stands out as one of the greatest models of friendship in the Bible. Jonathan was the eldest son of King Saul, and so heir to the throne of Israel. He demonstrated his prowess in battle and his bold leadership by overcoming a large Philistine garrison with only his armor-bearer at his side. He looked to be the ideal candidate for taking over the kingship. But God, through the prophet Samuel, anointed David to be the next king: "Then Samuel took the horn of oil, and anointed him in the midst of his brothers; and the Spirit of the LORD came mightily upon David from that day forward" (1 Sam 16:13, RSV). In sharp contrast to Jonathan, David was the youngest son of Jesse, a shepherd boy who had no claim to position or rule. He came to serve in the house of Saul and showed great courage and leadership by besting Goliath, the great warrior of the Philistines.

In natural terms, Jonathan and David should have been jealous rivals, not best of friends. But unaccountably this did not happen. Instead, "the soul of Jonathan was knit to the soul of David, and Jonathan loved him as his own soul" (1 Sam 18:1, RSV). This is the classic language of friendship—souls knit to one another in a profound bond. To cement this friendship, Jonathan makes a covenant with David. He strips himself of his own robe, armor, sword, and bow and gives them to David. Why? Because Jonathan loved David as he loved himself. This is stunning. Jonathan divested himself of his own future position and symbolically put David in his place. Whether he knew of David's anointing as king or simply intuited that David was the chosen one of the Lord, Jonathan served his friend David to his own detriment.

This friendship had to suffer through significant trials. Saul came to view David as his rival to the throne and repeatedly sought to kill him. Though Jonathan was loyal to his father, he would not cooperate in Saul's plots, but rather reconciled David and Saul (for a time). When Jonathan realized that his father was once again seeking David's life, he met with David, embraced him, and helped him to escape. The narrator tells us that "Jonathan made David swear again by his love for him; for he loved him as he loved his own soul" (1 Sam 20:17, RSV). Jonathan realized that he was aiding and abetting the man who would supplant him as king, but his fear of the Lord and his love for David caused him to lay down his own life for the sake of his friend. When David realized that Jonathan was putting his own life in jeopardy, he "fell on his face to the ground, and bowed three times; and they kissed one another, and wept with one another" (1 Sam 20:41, RSV). Secure in the covenant of friendship they had sworn to each other, they departed in peace. One last time Jonathan sought David and assured him of God's plan for his life. He told David not to fear, for Saul would fail to kill him and he would be the next king in Israel, with Jonathan serving at his side (1 Sam 23:17).

In the end it was not to be so. Jonathan died on the battlefield with his father and brothers. David mourned and sang a hymn in Jonathan's memory, recounting the great love between them as brothers and friends: "I am distressed for you, my brother Jonathan; very pleasant have you been to me; your love to me was wonderful, passing the love of women" (2 Sam 1:26, RSV). This is not a confession of homosexual love as many today conclude. This is the heartfelt love of one friend for another, potential rivals who had become brothers. We can rejoice that now, in the presence of the Lord, their friendship finds its true fulfillment and perfection.

·✦·

CHAPTER EIGHT

Friendship and Communion with God

We regard falling from God's friendship as the only thing dreadful and we consider becoming God's friend the only thing worthy of honor and desire. This, as I have said, is the perfection of life.

—Gregory of Nyssa[1]

There is nothing more beautiful than to be surprised by the Gospel, by the encounter with Christ. There is nothing more beautiful than to know him and to speak to others of our friendship with him.

—Benedict XVI[2]

---

[1] Gregory of Nyssa, *Life of Moses*, trans. Abraham J. Malherbe and Everett Ferguson, *Classics of Western Spirituality* (New York: Paulist, 1978), 320.

[2] Pope Benedict XVI, *Homily of His Holiness Benedict XVI for the Inauguration of His Pontificate* (April 24, 2005), available from http://www.vatican.va.

WE ARE NOT THE CLONE ARMY

To begin, I would like to pose a basic question about the subject of this book: What is the *point* of this great and costly adventure of discipleship we have been exploring? Why is it that Jesus issues a call to follow him, to deny our very lives, and to take up our cross? Is it because there is a job to be done and our help is needed, like soldiers enlisting in an army? Is it because we need to prove ourselves and come through some kind of test to be found worthy of a reward? Well, there is some truth to be found in these answers, but they don't get to the heart of the matter. We are called by God into the adventure of the Gospel because of love, because we were created for communion with God—the Father, Son, and Spirit. From the beginning, we were made to enter a freely-chosen friendship with our God, the source of our life. This is why God made us. This is why he took such steps—like becoming a man and dying for us—to redeem us when we had fallen from that friendship. This is why we are invited to walk with Jesus and our fellow disciples on a path of adventurous discipleship. All this is producing in us even now a life-giving communion with God that will reach its fulfillment in the age to come.

We are not being asked to do something that God himself, in Christ, has not already done. The words of 1 John ring out at this point: "In this the love of God was revealed among us, that God sent his only begotten Son into the world, so that we might live through him. In this is love, not that we loved God but that he loved us and sent his Son to be the atoning sacrifice for our sins" (1 John 4:9–10). Christ Jesus invites us to walk with him on a path he has already taken. This is why the Letter to the Hebrews urges us to run with endurance and perseverance the race that lies before us, and to keep our eyes on Jesus who pioneered and perfected the path of faith. Because of the joy that he saw ahead of him, he was able to endure the cross (Heb 12:1–2). We are called to do the same. This is why Paul calls us to "walk in love, as Christ loved us and gave himself for us" (Eph 5:2, RSV). The pilgrimage path of the disciple has already been trodden by Christ and by "so great a cloud of witnesses" who have gone before us (Heb 12:1).

It is critical to know that our God did not create us to be something like his Clone Army, like the Stormtroopers of *Star Wars* fame. Our God is not looking for worker bees to do a job or for servants to amuse and entertain him. In the Clone Army, each figure is just like the next, clad in the same armor and indistinguishable from all the others. If one falls, it makes no difference—more can be produced. In contrast to the Clone Army, each one of us is uniquely created and precious to God; none of us is replaceable by another. And our salvation—our eternal life—consists in this love and communion with God and one another. Living the adventure of discipleship is the divinely appointed way of entering and deepening this communion of love and friendship.

Our friendship with God is always personal but never isolated or individualistic. To be drawn into the costly adventure of discipleship is to be joined to a company of friends, a people, a society that we do not choose—it is chosen for us by the one who calls us. Again, the First Letter of John radiates the truth here: "What we have seen and heard we also proclaim to you, so that you may have fellowship with us. And our fellowship is with the Father and with his Son Jesus Christ" (1 John 1:3). John is proclaiming the Gospel of Jesus Christ, and this proclamation brings about a "fellowship"—the Greek word is *koinonia* and can be translated as "communion." The Gospel proclamation brings about unity with one another in the unity of the Father, Son, and Spirit. If we are not ready to sign up for friendship and communion with our fellow disciples, and love them accordingly, then we are not going to be able to have friendship and communion with God.

John goes on to state the goal in the most breathtaking terms: "See what love the Father has given us, that we should be called children of God; and so we are. . . . Beloved, in the present time we are God's children; it has not yet been revealed what we shall be, but we know that when he is revealed we shall be like him, for we shall see him as he is" (1 John 3:1–2). We are not identical clones, but God's children. This is what we are *right now*; what we will become is far too marvelous to put into words, but we know that we shall be "like him." Just as in human friendship, the friends begin to share a likeness to one another, so it is to a greater extent with divine friendship. In this case, however, it is we who become like God (and not the other way round). As Paul says, "And all of us, with unveiled faces, beholding the glory of the Lord, are being changed into the same image from one degree of glory to another" (2 Cor 3:18). This is why the Christian tradition uses such daring language as "divinization" and "deification" to describe our destiny: not that we merge into God, like into some colossal lava lamp, but that in our full and free personalities we become increasingly like God, sharing in his life, being changed into his likeness and image, and living in genuine friendship and communion with him. According to the Second Letter of Peter, in Christ we are privileged to become "partakers of the divine nature" (2 Pet 1:4, RSV).

FRIENDSHIP WITH GOD EXPLORED

The idea of being a friend of God goes all the way back to the Old Testament. Moses is marked out as the particular friend of God because of his intimacy with the Lord: "Thus the LORD used to speak to Moses face to face, as one speaks to a friend" (Exod 33:11, NRSVCE). The Letter of James tells us that Abraham, for his part, was also a friend of God. Abraham believed God's word to him, and this faith-filled reception was counted as righteousness for Abraham. And so he was called a friend of God (Jas 2:23). What do Moses and Abraham have in common? God spoke to them directly and they spoke with God in turn. They not only listened to God and obeyed, but they *conversed* with the Lord, often making strong demands upon him. The Lord revealed his mind to them, and they in turn made their thoughts and hopes known to the Lord.

From the Wisdom literature of the Old Testament, we learn that friendship with God is available to all. Psalm 25 says that "the friendship of the LORD is for those who fear him, and he makes known to them his covenant" (Ps 25:14, RSV) The Book of Wisdom declares that divine wisdom itself finds a home in holy people and causes them to become God's friends: "in every generation she passes into holy souls and makes them friends of God" (Wis 7:27, NRSVCE).

This idea of being called "the friend of God" does not appear directly in the New Testament. Instead, we learn that we become friends of God by becoming friends of Christ, who is the Son of God, "true God from true God." Friendship with Christ first appears in the life of John the Baptist. He identifies himself as the "friend of the bridegroom" who gladly steps aside so that the bride (that is, the Church) may be joined to her true bridegroom (that is, Christ). As the friend of Christ, John rejoices at the bridegroom's voice and is able to say, "He must increase, but I must decrease" (John 3:30).

The invitation to become Christ's friends, offered to his intimate disciples, comes from Jesus himself. On the day before he suffered, he revealed his love for his disciples and called them to imitate that love: "No one has greater love than this, to lay down one's life for one's friends" (John 15:13, NRSVCE). Jesus is on the verge of laying down his life for them (and for us all) and he calls them to do the same. Then he invites them to consider themselves no longer just servants and followers but genuine friends of the master. Servants aren't told what their master is planning—they just have to follow instructions. But Jesus calls the disciples his "friends" because he reveals to them what he is doing and includes them in his mission (John 15:14–15). This is a remarkable invitation! The disciples of Jesus, who listen to his voice and obey his word, are raised up to be his friends. What is the sign of this friendship? That he tells them what he is doing and reveals the Father's plan to them. Jesus brings his tested disciples into the intimacy of friendship.

But he does more than just this. He also promises that he will remain with them in a special way, by coming to dwell within them and make his home with them: "If anyone loves me, he will keep my word, and my Father will love him, and we will come to him and make our home with him" (John 14:23, ESV). How will it come about that both the Father and the Son will make their home within each disciple? This is made possible through the gift of the indwelling Spirit. Jesus promises the disciples that he will pray to the Father, and in answer the Father will give them "another Counselor" who will remain with them forever. Who is this other Counselor? It is the Holy Spirit, the Spirit of truth. Christ assures them that in that day they will know the Spirit, and the Spirit will dwell with them and be in them (John 14:16–17).

The intimate friendship that we have with God comes about through the dwelling of the Trinity—Father, Son, and Spirit—in the soul of the believer. We don't need to travel across the world and wait in long lines to have a few precious moments in the presence of Jesus. He has made it possible for each of us to be his friends, and friends of his Father, through the gift of the indwelling Spirit. Of course Jesus is present to us in many ways, preeminently in the Eucharist, but when he invites the disciples to be his friends, he links this directly to his coming to dwell within them through the Spirit.

Friendship with God finds a resounding echo in the tradition of our great teachers. Pope Gregory the Great (seventh century) stands amazed at the great gift of this

THE ADVENTURE OF DISCIPLESHIP

divine friendship: "How great is our Creator's mercy! We were unworthy servants, and he calls us friends. How great is our human value, that we should be friends of God!"[3] Cyril of Alexandria (fifth century) praises this friendship as one of the greatest gifts we have received: "And what could be thought greater, what could anyone say is more glorious than being called and being a friend of Christ?"[4] Thomas Aquinas (thirteenth century) says that "by the Holy Spirit we are established as friends of God," and that "it is evident that charity is the friendship of man for God."[5]

In our own day, the topic of friendship with God has received new emphasis. In his inaugural homily as pope, Benedict XVI praised the beauty of friendship with Christ with these words: "Only in this friendship are the doors of life opened wide. Only in this friendship is the great potential of human existence truly revealed. Only in this friendship do we experience beauty and liberation."[6] Pope Francis likewise identifies friendship with God as the mature expression of our encounter with the love of God:

---

[3] Gregory the Great, *Hom. in Evang.* 27.4, in David Hurst, trans., *Forty Gospel Homilies* (Kalamazoo: Cistercian Publications, 1990), 214.

[4] Cyril, *Commentary on John 15:14–15*; in Cyril of Alexandria, *Commentary on John*, vol. 2, trans. David R. Maxwell, *Ancient Christian Texts* (Downer's Grove, IL: IVP Academic, 2015), 231.

[5] Aquinas, *Summa contra Gentiles*, IV.20.5; *Summa Theologiae* II–II, q. 23, a. 1, trans. Fathers of the English Dominican Province (New York: Benziger, 1947–1948), https://www.ccel.org/ccel/aquinas/summa/home.html.

[6] Benedict XVI, *Homily for the Inauguration of His Pontificate.*

Thanks solely to this encounter—or renewed encounter—with God's love, which blossoms into an enriching friendship, we are liberated from our narrowness and self-absorption. We become fully human when we become more than human, when we let God bring us beyond ourselves in order to attain the fullest truth of our being. Here we find the source and inspiration of all our efforts at evangelization. (EG 8)

When we encounter the living God, we encounter his love, and this love is meant to grow into a mature and life-giving friendship. From the midst of this friendship comes our motivation and love to bring the good news of Jesus to others.

The preacher of the papal household, Raniero Cantalamessa, offers penetrating words on the greatness of the friendship that Christ extends to each of us. He begins by regretting that Christians often miss the invitation to be a friend of Christ: "Unfortunately, Jesus is rarely thought of as a friend and confidant." Why not? Because we tend to treat him as risen, ascended, and now no longer really accessible in this intimate way. He explains: "We forget that being 'true man,' as the dogma says—and even being the very perfection of humanity itself—he possesses the capacity for friendship to the highest degree, which is one of the noblest characteristics of a human being. It is Jesus who wants that relationship with us." During his earthly life, Jesus befriended only a few, but "now that he is risen and is no longer subject to the limitations of the body . . .

he offers every man and woman the possibility of having him as a friend in the fullest sense of that word."[7]

What this friendship with Christ (and so with God) looks like will be different for each of us. But let me offer the following three qualities of friendship with Christ that I have gleaned from the Scriptures and from the testimony of the tradition, as well as from my own experience. First, friendship with Jesus Christ means that we have known and encountered him personally—and continue to do so. This ongoing encounter may have a strong emotional impact, but this is not necessary or essential to genuine friendship. In fact, as time goes on, the encounter may grow deeper while the emotions grow quieter. It is also true, however, that friendship with Jesus Christ does *not* mean that we stop relating to him as God, with reverence and obedience. It is the Spirit who teaches us how to be reverent and intimate with God at the same time. We come to know Jesus intimately and personally, but we also revere him as true God. The disciples *after* the Resurrection are the best model for us here. Think of how they relate to him in the Upper Room or on the seashore eating a meal of flame-broiled fish.

Second, friendship with Jesus Christ means that we relate to him as a companion, one who is side-by-side with us. God in Christ has come down to us—he has taken on our nature and spoken to us in our language. And he continues to do this with his friends. As the Gospel of John tells us, to have friendship with Jesus is to know that

---

[7] Raniero Cantalamessa, *Fourth Lenten Homily* (April 4, 2014), https://zenit.org/articles/father-cantalamessa-s-4th-lent-homily-2014.

he is "within" us and that he dwells among us. As Jesus said plainly to his disciples, this means that he speaks his mind to us—he tells us things—and we listen to him. We revere his word. Further, we have boldness as the disciples did to speak to him and we even dare to ask great things of him. As we see in Abraham, Moses, and the saints, the friends of God feel free to express their thoughts, cares, and concerns. They "wrestle" with God in prayer because they know and love him.

Third and finally, friendship with Jesus Christ means that we know his love for us and that we are ready to lay down our lives for him. This friendship means giving our lives away for him and his "friends"—our fellow disciples. Friends don't just speak to each other—they love each other. And the primary way that Jesus loved us is that he laid down his life for us, his friends. As Pope Francis reminds us, this friendship with Jesus Christ means that we want others to enter into this friendship as fully as we have. There is no place for envy or jealousy in this friendship. Friendship with Jesus Christ leads to mission: we want to see others also enter into this friendship with him. This is why truly growing in friendship with the Father and Son through the Spirit is not only the height of spiritual perfection (as Gregory of Nyssa says) but also a great spur to mission.

TWO STORIES COMPARED: *LOST* AND *THE LAST BATTLE*

It is challenging to find examples or illustrations of friendship with God in adventure stories. Why this is the case should be obvious. Most adventure stories deal with human realities—or at least with created beings (like aliens from other planets). But in order to display friendship with God, God himself actually has to be one of the characters in the story who can relate as a "friend" to others. It is immensely difficult to bring God into the story as one of the characters without making God seem somehow less than God. Usually the best we can do is to show the providential action of God in the story—but this does not directly reveal what *friendship* with God might look like.

To illustrate something about "friendship" or "communion" with God (or the divine), I have chosen two adventure stories that would appear at first glance to be utterly dissimilar: the TV series *Lost* and C. S. Lewis's *The Last Battle*. But upon further inspection, the two have many similarities. Both aim to explore the purpose or meaning of life and both depict a final battle or struggle that leads to an "afterlife" and an encounter with the divine.

Lost ran for six seasons (121 episodes) and was one of the most popular and talked about programs of its day, garnering between ten to fifteen million viewers for each season. The basic plot centers around a plane crash on a desert island and the adventures that befall the survivors of the crash. Combining an intoxicating mix of human drama, science, mythology, time travel, and the supernatural, *Lost* dramatizes basic questions of human existence: Why are we here? What actually is real or true? Is there such a thing as "goodness" and does it matter if we are good? And finally, is our world reducible to material realities alone (pure science) or is there a spiritual reality, perhaps even a God, that is active in our lives? I will focus only on the final episode of the program in which many of the threads of the story are tied together and the grand finale is revealed.

The long and winding narrative boils down to a final confrontation between the evil figure, the so-called "smoke monster," and the main character (Jack) and his friends. Through bravery and cleverness, Jack and his companions finally manage to kill the evil figure and restore the island to its power and stability, thus in some sense saving the world. At the same time this is happening, the story moves to the mainland where these very same characters (and others from previous episodes) are one-by-one waking up to who they really are in their island identities and relationships, and they begin gathering in a local church building. As the audience, we are perplexed by all this—as the characters themselves are—but expect to be soon enlightened.

The striking thing about this final episode of *Lost* is how much the events and imagery draw on religious, and specifically Christian, symbols. Jack is a kind of Christ-figure who voluntarily takes upon himself the task of defeating the smoke monster, knowing that he will die in the effort. Just before the end, he says to Desmond, "I'll see you in another life, brother." He willingly sacrifices his life for this great cause, because that is what he is supposed to do, while his companions mourn and weep for him.

Meanwhile, back at the church on the mainland, all the main characters are gathering together. Ben and John, who have been at odds throughout the whole story, talk outside the church. To our surprise, Ben—who was one of the leading *evil* figures for much of the series—repents to John, saying that he was jealous and selfish and in the wrong. And John forgives him. A remarkable case of clear repentance. But then as John invites him to enter the church, Ben says that he still has things he needs to work out, so he's not coming in yet. Ben has chosen, appropriately, a self-imposed purgatory. He will (probably) eventually enter the church, but he needs to work on things—to get things straight—before he is ready for this.

At the same time, Jack has entered the back of the church where the casket of his father has been placed. Jack enters the chapel, which is adorned with crosses and Christian religious symbols, and opens the casket, only to find it empty. And then his father strides into the room alive, risen from the grave. It is a moving scene of the reunion of father and son. His father admits that he has died, but then Jack realizes that he, too, has died. Jack then wonders why all the people are gathered and where they are going. His father says that they are not leaving, but rather "moving on." Jack asks, "Where are we going?" His father responds, "Let's find out." The final scene in the church presents (in slow motion) the affectionate reunion of all the characters, now with Jack included— they are hugging and greeting and expressing affection. Finally, Jack's father pushes open the doors at the front of the church and a bright light appears and overshadows everyone until we can no longer see the characters—they have been swallowed up into the light.

Lost presents a final battle, a sacrificial death, and a reuniting of the beloved characters in an afterlife of joy, affection, and glory. All that they suffered is now taken up and made right in this reconciliation and peace that they find together. Neither they nor the audience know exactly what they are moving on to. But the bright light that encompasses them speaks of an entrance into the "divine"— whatever this may prove to be. There are many Christian elements in this story, especially about the end times and the beginning of a new world. But one figure is notably missing—Christ himself. Jack may be a Christ-like figure, but he is certainly not the source and center of the new life they are experiencing. *Lost* contains many of the elements of a Christian view of life, but it lacks the source and center: a personal God who has called everyone into personal friendship and communion. The best it can offer is a bright light and a hopeful expectation to "go and find out" what might be waiting for them.

C. S. Lewis's *The Last Battle* also presents a narrative of a final struggle that leads to the end of the world. A rising tide of evil and misfortune has overtaken Narnia. Tirian, the last king, and his faithful companion, Jewel the unicorn, demonstrate a profound personal friendship and show great loyalty to Aslan through these final events. Jill and Eustace return to Narnia to strengthen and accompany these companions in their final struggle. The plot hinges around the reported appearance of Aslan: Is this the real Aslan, coming forth from a stable, issuing what seem to be evil and dreadful commands? And if not, then where is the real Aslan and why is he allowing an imposter to enslave Narnia? In fact, as the readers know all along, this is a false Aslan, but nonetheless many of the Narnians are confused and led astray. At issue is really the question of basic loyalty: where is the real Aslan and how is one to prove faithful to him? In the midst of these disastrous events, King Tirian and Jewel keep faith with Aslan, with Jewel calling them all to bravery: "Now nothing remains for us seven but to go back to Stable Hill, proclaim the truth, and take the adventure that Aslan sends us."[8]

The climax hinges around a small stable, the abode where Aslan is said to be dwelling. To the great surprise and dread of the leading "bad" characters, the evil god Tash actually shows up in the stable—and devours them. At the same time, the true Aslan also appears and greets his faithful who have come through the battle and into the stable. With utter amazement, they discover that the stable contains within it a whole new world. "It is far bigger inside than it was outside."[9] The final chapters describe the end of Narnia, the final judgment of all its inhabitants, and the beginning of eternal life in the new and real Narnia. In the process, every creature comes face to face with Aslan and receives a judgment, either veering off into darkness or entering into the glory of Aslan's land.

Just as in *Lost*, all the beloved characters from the Narnia stories are reunited at the end. They, too, have died and experience great joy and wonder in this meeting of all the friends of Narnia through the ages. But then something happens that we don't find in *Lost*: the Christ-figure, Aslan, appears as the true center of their joy. Here is how Lewis describes Aslan's arrival in the midst of the gathered friends:

---

[8] C. S. Lewis, *The Last Battle* (New York: HarperCollins, 1984), 114.
[9] Lewis, *The Last Battle*, 223.

The sweet air grew suddenly sweeter. A brightness flashed before them. All turned. Tirian turned last because he was afraid. There stood his heart's desire, huge and real, the golden lion, Aslan himself, and already the others were kneeling in a circle round his forepaws and burying their hands and faces in his mane as he stooped his great head to touch them with his tongue. Then he fixed his eyes upon Tirian, and Tirian came near, trembling, and flung himself at the Lion's feet, and the Lion kissed him and said, "Well done, last of the Kings of Narnia who stood firm at the darkest hour."[10]

Aslan then greets and addresses the gathered friends personally. In the midst of their joy in each other and the delight of the new world, Aslan is their surpassing joy—he is the true center without which all the other joys and delights would remain fragmented and incomplete. The new world without the great lion would in a sense be nothing at all. He is what gives this world its glory and excellence; it is his presence that brings true joy to all.

Aslan then races off and shouts over his shoulder, "Come further in! Come further up!"[11] As they pursue him, marvels unfold; the friends learn more about this new land and their new bodies. In the words of Jewel: "I have come home at last! This is my real country! I belong here. This is the land I have been looking for all my life,

---

[10] Lewis, *The Last Battle*, 181.
[11] Lewis, *The Last Battle*, 195.

though I never knew it till now."¹² Even as they crest the ridge into the inner sanctum of this new land, Aslan appears once again, and all attention is turned toward him:

> The light ahead was growing stronger. . . . And then [Lucy] forgot everything else, because Aslan himself was coming leaping down from cliff to cliff like a living cataract of power and beauty. . . . And as He spoke, He no longer looked to them like a lion; but the things that began to happen after that were so great and beautiful that I cannot write them.¹³

Lewis closes the story at this point, for he does not have the words to describe this beatific vision: the glory of what we will see when we come face to face with the "Lord God Almighty and the Lamb" (Rev 21:22). But we do know that in that day our joy will be full (John 15:11) and that "we shall be like him, for we shall see him as he is" (1 John 3:2).

What *Lost* presents is impressive: a moral universe with right and wrong, a sense of the supernatural and life-after-death, a rendition of heaven, hell (and even purgatory), and a joyful reunion of friends after the hard labors in this life. But what it lacks is a personal God—the *person* of Christ—the center of all these things. This is precisely what *The Last Battle* displays: hard struggles and the proving of one's loyalties, great friendship both during and after the battles, the judgment of all and the

¹² Lewis, *The Last Battle*, 211.
¹³ Lewis, *The Last Battle*, 226–28.

end of the world—and a glorious picture of how each of the characters finds their joy in the friendship and love they have for Aslan.

GROWING IN FRIENDSHIP WITH GOD

The good news is that friendship with God is available to us in this life. We don't have to wait until we die and see the Lord in the next life. *Communion with God begins even now.* Of course we are beginners: we all have a lot to learn and we will never get to the "bottom" of friendship with God in this life. But because God has loved us and reached out by his grace to call us to himself—it is always his initiative—each of us can enter into genuine friendship with him. Through faith and Baptism, we are made new. God sanctifies us and comes to make his home within us through the Holy Spirit. And on the path of the costly adventure of discipleship, we are given access to the means of grace so that we can grow in this friendship.

Much could be said about the means of grace that contribute toward our growth in friendship with God. Here I want to speak about three "avenues" or "means" that help us to grow in this divine friendship. But before naming these, let's recall that the Father and Son have come and made their home in us through the Holy Spirit. The Catechism identifies the Spirit as "the interior Master of life according to Christ, a gentle guest and friend who inspires, guides, corrects, and strengthens this life" (1697). The Spirit, then, is the primary one who leads us into deeper friendship with God.

The first "avenue" to friendship with God is found in the Scriptures. In the Bible we find the entire narrative of salvation laid out before us. We learn who God is and how he acts, and we see his interactions with his "friends" throughout the ages. We can grow in our own friendship with God by getting to know him through regular reading of the Bible. "For in the sacred books, the Father who is in heaven meets His children with great love and speaks with them."[14] Reading the Bible prayerfully with faith enables us to know God more fully and opens up a conversation with him through which our friendship and communion with him will grow.

The second "avenue" is spending time with God in personal prayer. The analogy with human friendship applies here: if we want to grow in friendship with someone, we have to spend time with that person—and we will *want* to spend time with that person. So it is with God our Father and with Christ: if we want to grow in our friendship with God, we will set aside time daily to be with him. St. Teresa of Avila, a master of the spiritual life, says, "For mental prayer in my opinion is nothing else than an intimate sharing between friends; it means taking time frequently to be alone with Him who we know loves us. In order that love be true and the friendship endure, the wills of the friends must be in accord."[15] Personal prayer can take many forms, but whether we pray in a chapel, or in our room, or while walking through the woods, spending time with God is crucial to our growth in friendship with him.

---

[14] Dogmatic Constitution on Divine Revelation *Dei Verbum* (November 18, 1965), § 21, available from http://www.vatican.va.

[15] Teresa of Avila, *The Book of Her Life*, 8.5, in *The Collected Works of St. Teresa of Avila*, vol. 1, 2nd ed., trans. Kieran Kavanaugh and Otilio Rodriguez (Washington, DC: Institute of Carmelite Studies, 1987), 96.

The third "avenue" is availing ourselves of the sacraments. By Baptism we are born into friendship with God; through Confirmation we are strengthened by grace and the Spirit for the spiritual journey. The Eucharist provides us with "food for the journey," so that like Elijah, we will not faint on the way. Thomas Aquinas underlines the place of the sacraments in strengthening us for the journey that lies before us:

> Now it is clear that just as generation is required for corporeal life . . . so likewise food is required for the preservation of life. Consequently, just as for the spiritual life there had to be Baptism, which is spiritual generation; and Confirmation, which is spiritual growth: so there needed to be the sacrament of the Eucharist, which is spiritual food.[16]

For Thomas, the Eucharist in particular "does for the spiritual life all that material food does for the bodily life, namely, by sustaining, giving increase, restoring, and giving delight."[17] For its part, the sacrament of Penance heals the wounds of sin that we receive on the journey and restores us to full friendship with God: "The great efficacy of Penance consists in this, that it restores us to the grace of God, and unites us to Him in the closest friendship."[18] In fact, the Catechism (1468) identifies friendship with

---

[16] Aquinas, *ST* III, q. 73, a. 1.
[17] Aquinas, *ST* III, q. 79, a. 1.
[18] *The Catechism of the Council of Trent*, trans. John A. McHugh and Charles J. Callan (Rockford, IL: Tan Books, 1982), 270.

God as the most precious of the blessings that we receive in this life as children of God.

The path of costly discipleship that lies before each of us is a *difficult* path: we can expect trials and setbacks and times of perplexity that press us well beyond our own resources. How can we be sustained in this difficult pathway? The Lord God provides many helps along the way, but two of the most precious and powerful are the friends that he gives us for the journey and the friendship with himself that he extends to us. May we know this friendship with God more and more as we press on in the costly adventure of discipleship!

* *Portrait* *
THE RECENT NORTH AFRICAN MARTYRS

Those who die for their faith in Jesus—the martyrs—have a special claim to being the friends of Christ. Jesus himself said that the greatest love we have for another—for our friends—is to lay down our lives for them. The martyrs of every age give ample witness to this love—this friendship—by laying down their lives for Christ. Pope John Paul II drew our attention to the fact that all Christians, coming from our various traditions, "have a common *Martyrology.* This also includes the martyrs of our own century, more numerous than one might think, and it shows how, at a profound level, God preserves communion among the baptized in the supreme demand of faith, manifested in the sacrifice of life itself."[19]

Evidence of this common share in the martyrs occurred in early 2015, when a video was released showing the beheading of twenty-one Coptic Christians along the Libyan coast of the Mediterranean Sea. Why were they killed? Simply because they were Christians and confessed to being so. Fellow Christians across the world, including Pope Francis, joined in mourning their deaths but also rejoiced in the power of their witness. In the words of Francis, "The blood of our Christian brothers is a witness that cries out. . . . If they are Catholic, Orthodox, Copts, Lutherans, it is not important: They are Christians. The blood is the same: It is the blood which

---

[19] Pope John Paul II, Encyclical Letter on Commitment to Ecumenism *Ut Unum Sint* (May 25, 1995), § 84, available from http://www.vatican.va.

confesses Christ."[20] For these twenty-one Coptic men, the adventure of discipleship ended suddenly and with great cost. It was probably not what any of them had planned. But to them was granted the great privilege to die for Christ—and so to prove themselves Christ's friends.

[20] Justin Worland, "Pope Francis Condemns ISIS Killing of Coptic Christians," *Time* (February 16, 2015), http://time.com/3710911/pope-coptic-christian-killing.

·❖·

Living the Adventure

We must go on and take the adventure that comes to us.

—King Tirian, *The Last Battle*[1]

THE Gospel of Jesus Christ is the true and real adventure of the world. All other adventures that we create or imagine are just so many reflections of this great adventure of the Gospel. The adventures that we love to read and watch and retell can illuminate aspects of this true adventure of the Gospel. Understanding the nature of the Christian adventure can enliven our imaginations, help us to see what it means to be faithful to Jesus Christ, and inspire us to set out (or continue) on the path of costly discipleship.

A summary of the main conclusions about the costly adventure of discipleship may prove helpful. Here I am condensing into a few sentences what I have developed at greater length in the previous eight chapters.

[1] C. S. Lewis, *The Last Battle*, 125.

- The costly adventure of discipleship is not something that we arrange or contrive, but it draws us in and sweeps us into itself. We are not the authors of the story that we are in: we cannot write our own script. To become a disciple of Jesus Christ means leaving behind everything else and entering onto the path marked out for us by God.

- To embrace this adventure of discipleship, we need a venturesome faith marked by joy that is ready to risk all for the sake of Christ.

- The adventure of discipleship is *costly*, and the cost we pay is our whole lives. We can follow this costly call only if we have had a personal encounter with the living Christ. By his grace—and with great joy—we are called to follow God's plan for our lives.

- Jesus is much more than a superhero. Through the Incarnation, the "author" of the story of our world actually became one of its characters. But he didn't come just to save us from our problems. He died and rose again to make us new and to transform us from within.

- We press ahead on the path of costly discipleship strengthened by hope in a providential God who watches over our steps, and we have the great comfort of the Holy Spirit as our internal guide along the way.

- To walk the path of discipleship means that we share in the trials and sufferings of Christ, with joy. No true adventure is without trial and suffering: so it is in the costly adventure of discipleship to Jesus Christ.

- Christian discipleship is meant to be marked by genuine friendships that provide help, strength, and joy on our common pilgrimage. Friendships in Christ are not merely instrumental but display a foretaste of the communion we will have with each other eternally. Christian discipleship is a school of friendship.

- What is the point of this costly adventure of discipleship? We are called by God into the adventure of the Gospel because of love, because we were created for communion with God—the Father, Son, and Spirit. Jesus raises his disciples to become his friends, and this friendship and communion with him is one of the greatest gifts we receive.

I am grieved by how many people today, especially among the young, are adopting a fundamentally materialistic view of the world. They have become effective agnostics or atheists. In this view, the world—and human life—is nothing more than a mindless, purposeless collision of atoms and molecules. All happens by chance, not by divine providence. We are the accidental product of a universe that has no purpose. There is no respect or regard for "nature" or for any sense of purpose in the world. No, we are left by ourselves to *construct* our own reality and to define life on our own terms. This grim, meaningless relativism is becoming more and more the underlying narrative of our time.

The Gospel of Jesus Christ offers a powerful antidote and rejoinder to this materialistic narrative. We are not here by accident but by divine purpose. I am not a purposeless being who must create my own reality and identity, but I am a child of God, known by God, redeemed by Christ, filled with the Spirit, and joined in friendship with others. Not only is there a purpose for my life, but there is a purpose and meaning for the whole world. And the narrative of this world—the true narrative—is one of adventure. We cooperate with this divine purpose fully when we hear and respond to the word of the Gospel and find new life in Christ. But this does not end the adventure; it is the true beginning that reaches its fulfillment in eternal life.

The task for each of us is to realize what this true adventure of costly discipleship is, and like people who jump into a flowing stream, to throw ourselves into this adventure with all of our strength and determination—or better, to see that we've *already* been thrown into this adventure and so join ourselves to following Christ and following his call. We are not meant to hide out in the adventures of others but to find in them the inspiration to embrace our own. With the help of the God who befriends us and is always with us, with the gifts of faith, hope, and love, and in company with the friends given as our companions, we are called to make our way forward adventurously until the author of this story calls us home.

No one says this better than Paul. He wholeheartedly embraced the costly adventure in Christ to which he was called, never looking back but pressing on to the end: to full communion with Christ and with the friends of God in eternal life.

Not that I have already attained this or that I am already perfect. But I press on to take hold of it because I have been taken hold of by Christ Jesus. Brethren, I do not consider that I have taken hold of it, but one thing I do: forgetting what lies behind and straining forward to what lies ahead, I press on toward the goal for the prize of the upward call of God in Christ Jesus. (Phil 3:12–14)

·✦·

Bibliography

Aelred of Rievaulx. *Spiritual Friendship*. Translated by Mary Eugenia Laker. Kalamazoo: Cistercian Publications, 1977.

Aquinas, Thomas. *Summa contra Gentiles*. Translated by Joseph Kenny. New York: Hanover House, 1955–1957. http://dhspriory.org/thomas/ContraGentiles.htm.

———. *Summa Theologiae*. Translated by Fathers of the English Dominican Province. New York: Benziger, 1947–1948. https://www.ccel.org/ccel/aquinas/summa/home.html.

———. *Commentary on the Gospel of John: Chapters 13–21*. Translated by Fabian Larcher and James A. Weisheipl. Washington, DC: Catholic University of America Press, 2010.

Aristotle. *The Nichomachean Ethics*. Translated by W. D. Ross. Oxford: Oxford University Press, 1998.

Austen, Jane. *Pride and Prejudice*. New York: E. P. Dutton, 1976.

Benedict XVI. *Homily of his Holiness Benedict XVI for the Inauguration of His Pontificate*. April 24, 2005.

———. *God is Love Deus Caritas Est*. December 25, 2005.

———. *The Sacrament of Charity Sacramentum Caritatis*. February 22, 2007.

———. *The Word of the Lord Verbum Domini*. September 30, 2010.

Bonhoeffer, Dietrich. *The Cost of Discipleship*. Revised ed. New York: MacMillan, 1979.

Cantalamessa, Raniero. *Fourth Lenten Homily*. April 4, 2014. https://zenit.org/articles/father-cantalamessa-s-4th-lent-homily-2014.

Catechism of the Council of Trent. Translated by John A. McHugh and Charles J. Callan. Rockford, IL: Tan Books, 1982.

Chesterton, G. K. *Heretics*. New York: John Lane, 1909.

Cyril of Alexandria. *Commentary on John*. Vol. 2. Translated by David R. Maxwell. *Ancient Christian Texts*. Downer's Grove, IL: IVP Academic, 2015.

De Sales, Francis. *Introduction to the Devout Life*. New York: Vintage Books, 2002.

_____ and Jane de Chantal. *Letters of Spiritual Direction*. Translated by Péronne Marie Thibert. Edited by Wendy M. Wright and Joseph F. Power. New York: Paulist, 1988.

Dogmatic Constitution on Divine Revelation *Dei Verbum*. November 18, 1965.

Francis. The Joy of the Gospel *Evangelii Gaudium*. November 24, 2013.

Gregory of Nyssa. *Life of Moses*. Translated by Abraham J. Malherbe and Everett Ferguson. *Classics of Western Spirituality*. New York: Paulist, 1978.

Gregory the Great. *Forty Gospel Homilies*. Translated by David Hurst. Kalamazoo: Cistercian Publications, 1990.

Hibberd, James. "A Dance with Dragons Interview," interview with George R. R. Martin. July 12, 2011. http://ew.com/article/2011/07/12/george-martin-talks-a-dance-with-dragons.

John Paul II. *Homily of His Holiness John Paul II for the Inauguration of His Pontificate.* October 22, 1978.

———. Encyclical Letter on Commitment to Ecumenism *Ut Unum Sint.* May 25, 1995.

———. Apostolic Letter *Novo Millennio Ineunte.* January 6, 2001.

Lepp, Ignace. *The Ways of Friendship.* Translated by Bernard Murchland. New York: MacMillan, 1966.

Lewis, C. S. "The Weight of Glory." June 8, 1942. http://www.verber.com/mark/xian/weight-of-glory.pdf.

———. *The Four Loves.* New York: Harcourt Brace, 1960.

———. *The Voyage of the Dawn Treader.* New York: HarperCollins, 1980.

———. *The Silver Chair.* New York: HarperCollins, 1981.

———. *The Horse and His Boy.* New York: HarperCollins, 1982.

———. *The Last Battle.* New York: HarperCollins, 1984.

Martin, George R. R. *A Game of Thrones.* New York: Bantam Books, 2011.

Newman, John Henry. "Lead Kindly Light" (1834). https://newmanu.edu/about-newman/history-of-newman/lead-kindly-light.

———. "The Ventures of Faith." *Parochial and Plain Sermons* (San Francisco: Ignatius Press, 1987), 914–21.

Pieper, Josef. *Faith, Hope, Love.* San Francisco: Ignatius Press, 1997.

Ravier, André. *Francis de Sales: Sage and Saint.* San Francisco: Ignatius Press, 1988.

Reno, R. R. "American Satyricon." *First Things* (October 2001). https://www.firstthings.com/article/2001/10/american-satyricon.

Rosen, Christine. "Virtual Friendship and the New Narcissism." *The New Atlantis* (Summer 2007): 15–31.

Smith, Christian and Melina Lundquist Denton. *Soul Searching: The Religious Lives of American Teenagers*. Oxford: Oxford University Press, 2005.

Smith, Christian and Kari Christoffersen. *Lost in Transition: The Dark Side of Emerging Adulthood*. Oxford: Oxford University Press, 2011.

Snow, Patricia. "Empathy is not Charity." *First Things* (October 2017). https://www.firstthings.com/article/2017/10/empathy-is-not-charity.

Stark, Rodney. *The Rise of Christianity*. San Francisco: HarperCollins, 1997.

Teresa of Avila. *The Book of Her Life*. In *The Collected Works of St. Teresa of Avila*. Vol. 1. 2nd ed. Translated by Kieran Kavanaugh and Otilio Rodriguez. Washington, DC: Institute of Carmelite Studies, 1976.

Tolkien, J. R. R. *The Hobbit*. Revised ed. New York: Ballantine Books, 1966.

_____. *The Fellowship of the Ring*. New York: Ballantine Books, 1965.

_____. *The Two Towers*. New York: Ballantine Books, 1965.

_____. *The Return of the King*. New York: Ballantine Books, 1965.

Vigneron, Allen H. *Unleash the Gospel*. June 3, 2017. http://www.unleashthegospel.org.

Weddell, Sherry A. *Forming Intentional Disciples: The Path to Knowing and Following Jesus*. Huntingdon, IN: Our Sunday Visitor, 2012.

Willard, Dallas. *The Divine Conspiracy: Rediscovering Our Hidden Life In God*. New York: HarperCollins, 1998.

Williams, Jerome K. *True Reformers*. Greenwood Village, CO: Augustine Institute, 2017.

Worland, Justin. "Pope Francis Condemns ISIS Killing of Coptic Christians." *Time*. February 16, 2015. http://time.com/3710911/pope-coptic-christian-killing.

Wright, Wendy. "'Hearts Have a Secret Language': The Spiritual Friendship of Francis de Sales and Jane de Chantal." *Vincentian Heritage Journal* 11 (1990): 45–58.

·✥·

Index of Biblical References

Genesis

3:15	101
12:1, 4	46
22:16-18	47

Exodus

3:10-11	17
4:1-13	17-18
33:11	169

Ruth

1:13	110
1:16-17	110
4:14	111

1 Samuel

16:13	161
18:1	161
20:17	162
20:41	162
23:17	162

2 Samuel

1:26	163

Psalms

1:3	43
25:14	169
42:5-6	42

Proverbs

6:9	40

21:25	41
26:14	41

Wisdom

7:27	170

Sirach

2:1	113

Matthew

1:5	111
2:13-18	117
4:8-9	21
4:18-24	2
5:1	52
5:10-12	113, 128
5:48	82
6:25-33	40, 88
7:28-29	53
8:19-22	54
9:9	2
13:44-46	44, 53
16:24	39
19:21-22	59
19:29-30	37
25:14-30	34
25:20-21	43
28:19-20	53

Mark

8:34-36	1, 54-55
12:28-31	52
14:36	62

Luke

1:29	27
1:35	27
1:38	27
2:35	27
4:1-2	128
5:4	30
7:37-38	65
7:47	65
14:28-30	59
16:13	39
22:28	129
22:46	129

John

1:1-3	21
1:14	21
3:16	82
3:17	51
3:30	170
6:60	62
6:68	62
10:10	83
12:24-26	56
14:2	39
14:16-17	108, 171
14:23	171
14:26	108

15:5	82
15:11	182
15:13-15	160, 170
16:33	66

Acts of the Apostles

9:1-9	2
9:15-16	113

Romans

5:5	51
5:7-8	82
8:14-17	42, 108
8:18	131
8:24-25	105
8:29	82
8:35	109

1 Corinthians

10:13	129
13:12	104

2 Corinthians

1:5	130
1:8-10	20, 130
3:4-5	43
3:18	168
4:8-9	130
4:16-17	131
5:17	82, 85
8:9	83

Galatians

2:20	24

Ephesians

2:1-3	80

5:2	167	3:1-2	168
6:12	117	3:8	117
Philippians		4:9-10	166
3:13-14	43, 192-93	5:11	83
4:6	88	**Revelation**	
4:7	88	12:17	117
4:13	42	14:4	127
Colossians		21:3-4	102
1:16	21	21:22	182
3:14	157		
2 Timothy			
3:12	129		
Hebrews			
4:16	42		
5:7-8	128		
11:1	33		
11:8	46		
12:1-2	131, 167		
James			
1:2-3	130		
1:12	122		
2:23	169		
1 Peter			
1:13	108		
4:12-13	130		
5:7	40		
2 Peter			
1:4	169		
2:19	66		
1 John			
1:3	168		

·✦·

INDEX OF SUBJECTS

Abraham, 21, 26, 33, 34, 46-47, 101, 169, 175

Acedia, 30, 31, 41, 107

Adventure

Anatomy of, 13-20

Gospel as the real, 11, 20-25, 189

Love of, 7-11, 70

Real and contrived, 11-20

Aelred of Rievaulx, 137, 144

Aquinas, Thomas, 139, 140, 172, 185

Aristotle, 135, 137, 139, 140, 141, 143

Austen, Jane, 138, 148-54

Baptism, 183, 185

Batman Begins, 75-77

Benedict XVI (Pope), 57-58, 69, 165, 172

Bible (Scriptures), 4, 20, 21, 26, 34, 161, 174, 183-84

Bonhoeffer, Dietrich, 49, 50-51

Cantalamessa, Raniero, 173-74

Captain America and the Winter Soldier, 77-79

Chesterton, G.K., 7, 14

The Church, 32, 50, 52, 60, 85, 170,

City Slickers, 10

Cross, 1, 39, 54-55, 56, 71, 86, 102, 126, 128, 131, 132, 166, 167

Crossroads, 57, 61-62, 63, 64, 66

Cyril of Alexandria, 172

Damien of Molokai (St.), 67-68

David (King), 21, 27, 101, 111, 161-63

De Chantal, Jane (St.), 138, 155-59

De Sales, Francis (St.), 138, 143, 144, 155-59

Discipleship

Cost of, 26, 49-52, 61,114

Intentional. 59-60

Joy of, 43-45

Sayings of Jesus, 51-55

Steps to, 56-63

Divinization (deification), 168-69

Eucharist, 126, 171, 185

Faith
  Entrusting, 32-33
  Venturesome, 33-43
Francis (Pope), 43-44, 52, 58, 172, 175, 187
Freedom (in Christ), 66, 94, 156
Friendship
  With others, 135-160
  With God, 165-186
Game of Thrones, 94-95, 98-101
God the Father, 22, 42, 49, 51, 61, 62, 81-82, 84, 88, 90, 108-109, 122, 128, 159, 166, 168, 171, 175, 183, 184, 191
Grace, 4, 19, 27, 29, 34, 49, 50, 52, 57, 60, 61, 64, 66, 84, 105, 108, 109, 114, 126-27, 129, 158, 183, 185, 190
Gregory of Nyssa, 165, 175
Gregory the Great (Pope St.), 171-72
The Hobbit, 9, 13, 14, 94
Holy Spirit, 25, 27, 41, 42, 51, 53, 57, 64, 81, 90, 102, 103, 105, 108-9, 127-28, 130, 132, 144, 157, 161, 166, 168, 171-72, 174, 175, 183, 185, 190, 191
Hope, 26, 36, 41-42, 45, 87, 89-90, 103-8, 109, 110-11, 114, 132, 190, 192

Incarnation, 69, 83-85, 190
John of the Cross (St.), 115, 133-34
John Paul II (Pope St.), 29, 30, 31, 187
John the Baptist, 170,
Jonathan (see David)
Lepp, Ignace, 135, 137, 140, 142, 143
Lewis, C. S., ix, 3-4, 9, 18-19, 24-25, 91, 94, 96, 119, 120, 122, 142, 159, 176, 179, 180, 182
The Lord of the Rings, 9, 17, 22, 94, 95, 97, 98, 103, 119, 123-25, 138, 141, 145-48
Lost, 175-180, 182
Martin, George R. R., 94-95, 98-101
Mary (Mother of God), 27-28, 102, 115
The Matrix, 10
Moses, 17-18, 21, 33, 101, 169, 175
Mother Teresa, 86
Narnia, Chronicles of, 9, 91, 92, 119
Newman, John Henry, 7, 29, 32, 33-37, 42
Nouwen, Henry, 156

Paul (the Apostle), 19-20, 24, 42-43, 80, 82, 88, 105, 129-30, 131, 157, 167, 168, 192

Peter (the Apostle), 1, 3, 30, 40, 55, 57, 62, 64, 71, 108, 130

Pieper, Josef, 87, 105-7

Potter, Harry, 9, 115

Prayer, 65, 71, 88, 175, 184

Pride and Prejudice, 148-154

Providence, 21, 23, 35, 87, 89-104, 109

Redemption, 69, 75, 80-83

Reno, R.R., 30-31

RoboCop, 72, 73, 83, 84

Rosen, Christine, 136

Ruth, 110-11

Sacraments, 185

Scriptures (see Bible)

Smith, Christian, 38, 79

Snow, Patricia, 131-32

Star Wars, 167

Stark, Rodney, 71

Suffering, 19, 20, 21, 51, 113-132

Superheroes (paradigm), 9, 69-70, 72-84, 190

Testing (see trials)

Tolkien, J. R. R., ix, 4, 9, 13, 15, 63, 94-98, 99, 100, 119, 124-27, 138, 145-48

Treasure Island, 8, 14, 16

Trials (testing), 19, 20, 105, 113-122, 127-131, 134, 162, 186, 190,

Vigneron, Allen, 58

Wright, Wendy, 155, 158